WHY CAN'T EVERYTHING JUST
STAY THE SAME?

≫→ *AND OTHER THINGS I SHOUT WHEN I CAN'T COPE*

STEFANIE PREISSNER

HACHETTE
BOOKS
IRELAND

First published in Ireland in 2017 by HACHETTE BOOKS IRELAND

First published in paperback in 2018

1

Cataloguing in Publication Data is available from the British Library.

ISBN 978 1 4736 6240 7

Typeset in ArnoPro and Kozuka by Bookends Publishing Services
Printed and bound in Great Britain by Clays Ltd, St Ives plc

Hachette Books Ireland policy is to use papers that are natural,
renewable and recyclable products and made from wood grown in sustainable
forests. The logging and manufacturing processes are expected to conform
to the environmental regulations of the country of origin.

Hachette Books Ireland
8 Castlecourt Centre
Castleknock
Dublin 15
Ireland

A division of Hachette UK Ltd
Carmelite House, 50 Victoria Embankment, EC4Y 0DZ

www.hachettebooksireland.ie

CONTENTS

*Some of the names and details in this book
have been changed to respect the privacy of individuals.*

For my nana,
for every chicken wing,
every Sunday crossword,
every warm summer night, eating chips in the mobile …

I love you so much.

INTRODUCTION

FEAR OF CHANGE ISN'T DELIVERED BY THE STORK
when you're dropped into your crib on day one. Fear of change
grows with you, germinates in uncertainty and thrives on
inconsistency. I don't fight to keep the walls of my life standing
up because I think it's fun, I fear change because I haven't
enjoyed many of the changes I have experienced.

My sense of security was obliterated as a kid. I can't quite say
for sure if it was the fact that my father left when I was less than
two, or the fact that, in that same year, Santa took my soother in
exchange for a Wendy house. Either way, my little foundations
were shaken to breaking point and the cracks that appeared
were quickly filled with a dense matrix of insecurity, fear of

change, anxiety about the unknown, wariness of the new and apprehension of danger.

I was born in Germany. People have often said that fact 'makes sense' when they get to know me. Maybe it's because I am direct, love rules and order, and live by the motto, 'Early is on time, on time is late and late is unacceptable' that people think I fit the Teutonic stereotype. I don't drink beer and I don't like football but, apart from that, like the Christmas tree, the hole punch and the coffee filter, I am 100 per cent 'Made in Germany'.

I don't really remember the move back to Ireland, but I imagine it like the film *Look Who's Talking* where the kid, Mikey, is born. He's happy out floating around the womb and then BAM, all of a sudden he's reefed out of it and he's cold and moist and screaming to be put back in. I mean, it can't have been *that* traumatic but it was definitely a rebirth. And it sent a need for stability flying out from me into the atmosphere of my life to orbit me eternally like a sort of personal solar system of trepidation.

As a kid, all of my board games were meticulously stored. Each small piece kept in a tiny clear plastic Ziploc bag, freed for the duration of the game and then replaced in its transparent cage until the Cluedo fancy took me again. All of my games retained their instructions and rule books. They were thumbed and dog-eared from reiterations to new players who had to be briefed on best practice before I would play with them.

Some grown-ups called me fussy or highly strung. In school, all my colouring pencils had to be sharpened to the same length and I would often tell the teacher if another kid was 'going too hard on my colours'. I didn't want to be a tell-tale but if the teachers insisted on cultivating a culture of 'sharing', then they should have to reconcile the fact that some kids actually care about keeping their things in order.

Amiright?!

Other adults called me 'hard work'. OK, so I admit that demanding that my grapes be deseeded was probably a bit much, but I had become accustomed to such comforts thanks to my nana. She wheeled me around as a baby, pushing the buggy with one hand and trying to remove seeds from green grapes with the other. This must have been before they learned to genetically modify grapes.

The more sympathetic adults in my life chose words like 'meticulous' to describe the way in which I would fold the tinfoil into little triangles when I had finished my crackers and Nutella at lunch-time. The truth is I was neither meticulous nor highly strung.

I was terrified.

It's exhausting and demanding being a kid. You never know if you're doing it right, except in situations where instructions are given very clearly and then you know for sure you're playing by the rules. Maybe that's why I spent so much time as a teenager in the swimming pool. There, the rules were laid out in plain black and white on the wall. There was no grey area.

No diving

No running on the deck

Swimming hats must be worn at all times

Shower before entering the pool

No shouting or horseplay

No petting

See? Very clear.

Although I do remember asking several coaches what 'petting' was and remained confused when they turned on their heels and moved eight feet away from me.

The happy embers in my youthful eyes which had been ignited by always being told what to do were extinguished when I moved into young adulthood. Suddenly, I was being given 'space to make mistakes', 'room to grow' and the dreaded 'freedom to find out who you are'. I had no interest. I didn't want the wayward, carefree, hobo, boho emancipation that most teenagers crave. How was I meant to know what was safe if no one told me? How was I meant to know if I was good if I didn't know what was bad? How can you win if you don't know the rules of the game?

I still maintain I earned £600 for my First Holy Communion. (Well, it was hardly 'earned' but 'made' seems so crass.) I think I remember walking into the credit union and lodging £510 having spent £90 on a jersey and a watch. My mother tells me I – outrageously – made nearly two times that.

Keep that in mind when you read this book. My memories are flawed, unreliable and sometimes just plain fictitious. They are real to me, but then I tell myself stories to make the world easier to process.

One time, I lost my wallet and I made up this whole story in my head that I had seen a homeless person on the street and had probably subconsciously dropped it just metres from him to help him find a warm place to stay for the night. It made the loss of my money and credit cards more palatable when I told myself that I had helped someone.

So, sit back, take a large pinch of salt and read on.

If you have any specific questions you can ask me on Twitter @stefpreissner. I may not answer immediately – I may be rocking in a foetal curl with the anxiety of public opinion looming down on me – but when I am brave enough, I will.

Thanks in advance.
Stef

1

GUIDES TO LIFE

I LOVE RULES.

I *love* them.

I can't stress this enough.

My surname – Preissner – comes from the word 'Prussia', which was a German kingdom that was famous for its unusually well-organised and effective army. It's not off the stones I licked it, like.

I am at my most calm and comfortable when I know exactly how everything works, what is expected, what is out of place and what exactly is going to happen. I suspect this is probably why I thrived in school but struggled with the freedom of university.

In school, the rules were very clear. They were even printed in our homework notebooks. These were general rules about listening, being on time and being respectful, but we had non-printed rules too. These 'addendum' rules were less clear but I followed them with the same vigour. We weren't allowed any unhealthy foods, although 1990s Ireland was hardly the leader of the global health trend – I don't think I heard of an avocado until I was twenty. We also had a rule against standing in a circle. In the yard, we weren't allowed to gather in a circle because, apparently, it was suspicious. There was no running in the yard either so my memory of primary school lunch-times is a sea of slow-moving children equidistant from one another in various geometric patterns.

In secondary school, the rules were equally restrictive and there were more of them, but I still enjoyed the buttressing they provided. On the list of basic school rules that hung on the wall in the hall, the caretaker had tacked on an addendum and, as the world moved into the twenty-first century, rules were added to make sure the school felt none of the progress that was happening outside of its sweaty, mint-green walls. The additions included, but I can guarantee are no longer limited to:

No piercings
No hair dye
Minimal make-up (and only for those with acne)
No nail polish

No rolled-up skirts

No phones

No gum.

Our school was quicker than most institutions at adapting to change. It seemed that our school had a rule against phones within hours of Nokia inventing the first one. The corridors of St Mary's in Mallow have never known the joy of a polyphonic ringtone.

In university, I was like a balloon freshly escaped from the grubby hand of a child. There were no rules, no regulations and I was free to drift whichever way the strongest force wanted me to go.

I'm really lucky I was never targeted by Opus Dei. I would have been prime Opus Dei material – just a lost regional girl looking for a sense of structure and guidance, which is not something that my Drama and Theatre Studies degree course prided itself on. In fact, I'm pretty sure that part of their ethos in course number CK112 was 'non-formal examinations'. They boasted a level of self-regulation with students being 'free to' and 'encouraged to' learn. I should have known earlier I would struggle. I should have opted for a course like Medicine where the prospectus uses words like 'demanding', 'disciplined', 'focus', 'rigorous' and even 'trauma' – in fairness, I reckon the trauma is more about the content of the lessons and less the experience of the course, but at least you know it's going to be hardcore and full of lovely rules and expectations.

I loved the eight hours a week I had in my course – it was

the other 160 free hours that I struggled with. Why was no one telling me where to be? Why did no one mind if I didn't show up? Why was there no one breathing down my neck, telling me that my shirt needed to be tucked in or that drinking eight coffees was too much?

On my first day at university, I remember the fear settling in as I looked around the massive UCC quadrangle and noticed that, apart from the blue graphic T-shirts, there was no other way to identify the shepherds from the sheep. There were no grown-ups. There were at least 1,500 people there and there were no more than five years between the oldest and the youngest. I remember queuing up for my induction package, which included a condom, twelve free pens and a Pot Noodle, thinking about Jeremy Myers. Jeremy was famous in Mallow because he'd had a thirteen-year-old babysitter when he was twelve, and everyone had mocked him and called him a baby. The first day in UCC was the same. We were all like Jeremy Myers. Children being babysat by children.

Rules, although they can be limiting, gave young me a definite sense that someone was in control and that I was safe. Even today, the normal rules of social conduct are like a gentle padding on the sharp edges of the world. Like, it's just a known fact that when you go to the cinema and there are lots of empty seats, you do not sit right next to someone, even if the seat number on your ticket instructs you to. This is an example of social rules overriding 'The Establishment'. I feel the same way about waiting for the green man at pedestrian lights when there are clearly no cars coming.

These are two examples on a very short list of rules where I let my common sense overrule the law of the land. Outside of them, I am extremely law-abiding, sometimes to my detriment. I have paid for a second ticket after missing my train when other people just walk confidently towards the track, pretending their ticket is for the next train. I have missed the Luas because I have been fumbling with change at the machine when other people just walk on without a ticket and risk it. I read magazines by starting with the table of contents – why do people just pick up a magazine and flick through? That's why the contents is there!

If I am in a new situation, I look for someone to give me rules. There is always someone more experienced around who can guide you towards what is acceptable in that context. You know, when you go to Nando's and they say, 'Welcome to Nando's, have you been with us before?', and, if you haven't, they sit you down and explain the whole menu and the ordering process and the fact that the drinks are 'bottomless' and that you can keep getting up for refills? I find that so comforting. You go in and someone takes the time to explain all the workings and rules of the new environment you're in. I always look for the equivalent of the Friendly Nando's Worker (FNW) in any situation.

The first time I came to Dublin after the Luas had been completed, I was in desperate need of an FNW to explain how the bloody thing operated. There wasn't one around, but still I continued my search. I ended up having the ticketing system of the new Dublin tram service explained to me by a homeless person who had been begging close to the ticket machine for enough days to have learned how it worked. Between buying the ticket and paying the homeless man for his help, and giving him extra out of guilt, I would have been better off getting a taxi. My point is, there's always an FNW somewhere, someone who knows more than you do, and they are useful and necessary.

I love IKEA. IKEA is an organised jumble of my favourite things: order, storage solutions and Swedish meatballs. The showrooms and market warehouse, with their neat rows and economic use of space, provide the comfort I remember getting from colouring inside the lines. The way it operates is so clear and direct, there are even arrows on the floor to show you what direction to walk in. Sometimes, you might catch barbarians walking against the flow of oncoming human traffic, each carrying a yellow bag filled with dish scrubbers and the odd lamp. These invidious patrons can ignite either fury or pity in me, depending on their facial expression. If they seem proud to be fomenting insurrection by marching against the grain, I give them a stare that would freeze magma, but their faces are more often etched with deep lines of anguish as they plough through the crowd, scrambling to get back to the shelf bracket they missed, knowing their entire four-hour trip will be pointless if they abandon it. To them, I tilt my head in pity. *You've obviously made some poor choices in your life, my friend, poor choices that have led you to this, and no amount of walking backwards can redeem you from your current hell.* And on I go.

IKEA and Nando's leave nothing to chance. That's why I love them. I do *not* love music festivals. Music festivals are too much of a free-for-all. There are too many variables and too few rules.

If I go to a music festival, how will I shower? If I bring baby wipes will someone else see that I have had the foresight to bring them and ask me to share – and then will I have enough? Where will I sleep safe in the knowledge that a drunk person isn't going to fall onto my tent in a stupor and crack my skull? If I get lost, how will I find my people? Will they be able to hear their phones over the noise? What if their batteries die, do they have chargers with them? Can I ask my friends not to use their phones just in case I get lost and need to ring them?

It's just easier for me and my friendships if I abstain from anywhere people go to 'let their hair down'. My hair is most often in a ponytail. Two bobbles. For slippage.

In a museum, I will ask a staff member what their policy is on touching the art – some places, like the Louvre, aren't too keen on it, but at the Tate it's fair game. In a restaurant, I want to know if it's table service or not. If it is table service, do I have to call the waiter over to pay or do I go to them? It can ruin a night if you think you have to go to the till to pay and then you go there and they tell you they will bring the machine to the table and then you come across as impatient and demanding and it's just terrible so it's just better to have rules so we all know what is expected.

As a kid, I loved people who could explain the ambiguity of the world to me. The adults with answers that lit up the obscurity of youth. At first, it was my mother and my nana.

When I was a very small child, between two and three years old, we spent time every weekend at my godmother's house. She had a stand-up piano in the sitting room. On my first day in the house, my eyes lit up when I saw it. I plodded towards the instrument to impress my captive audience, but my mother told me the piano was locked and wouldn't open. I was so obedient and rule-compliant that I was seventeen before I found out that the piano had never been locked. It didn't even have a lock. It had been open all that time and I just took it as gospel that it was locked.

My mother and my grandmother were able to explain house rules and family expectations. They taught me that shirts had to be ironed, visitors had to see me in clean clothes when they arrived (if I got dirty while they were there that was OK), and cursing was fine as long as I wasn't cursing at them.

When I got older, the world opened up to me in all of its strangeness, and the variations and diversity of what was acceptable was overwhelming. It started at Emer Reidy's house when I was ten and three quarters.

I visited her house for a sleepover, my first sleepover – and my last that didn't take place at my house. I remember being really disturbed by the difference in rules in my friend's house. In Emer's house, we weren't allowed upstairs until it was time for sleep, we were only allowed to sit on the edge of the couch so as not to disturb the plumped-up cushions, and we had to eat pizza with cutlery and at the table with the television off. We were reading *The Diary of Anne Frank* in school at the time, and Emer's mother wouldn't let her read two books at once so when we were going to sleep, she read aloud from 'The Diary' and I remember relating to the trapped girl in the attic that night more than I should have.

I did not like *those* rules.

They didn't make sense to me. Couches are for sitting on, bedrooms are for playing in and pizza is a finger food! Who has white, high-pile carpet and a ten-year-old? Insanity. I can't remember many other details because I never went back to Emer's house again, and vowed that any other sleepovers that I was attending were going to be hosted by me. Then, there were friends whose houses seemed to have no rules. Cats, cat hair and food flakes of unknown provenance littered the rugs and furniture, and the arms of the couch were threadbare from kids jumping off them.

There is nothing more disconcerting than having two conflicting rules in a certain situation. Are you allowed to run up the slide or not? Because some parents are OK with it and some parents say no to it.

Why am I allowed to wear my shoes in my house but when I go to my aunt's I have to take them off?

Why in the weeks leading up to Easter is chocolate a sin?

why do capital letters at the start of sentences matter so much?

Will the raw eggs in cake mixture really give me salmonella or are people just trying to stop me from living my life?

Over the years, I have asked these questions of various adults and it seems that everyone has different answers. Some adults let me run up the slide when I asked, and then I hated them. If adults let me run up the slide, I lost all respect for them. How could I respect them when they obviously didn't know the rules or, worse again, they knew them but they weren't interested in keeping them?

There were heaps of rules at Mass. When to stand, when to sit, that you had to be quiet, when to shake hands and what to say. It was like a well-oiled machine. And that was before you even learned the commandments. My cousins and I had always been told to obey the rules at Mass – told by teachers, parents, family, nuns and priests. It seemed like the whole world was in harmonious agreement over one thing – you obey the rules at Mass. And then the Sunday of the Silverstone Grand Prix came along when Michael Schumacher was in pole position. I didn't know what that meant, but my family were *big* into motor racing. Mass wasn't going to end until 12:45 p.m. at the earliest, the exact time the grand prix was starting. Just before Communion, my uncle, who had been getting more and more impatient at the length of the sermon, leaned over and whispered something in my ear. This was the first rule broken. I was so shocked that he was breaking the rules that I didn't hear what he said. Then he leaned over to my cousin and whispered something to him and, instantly, my cousin burst into tears. My uncle picked him up and carried him out of the church. My other cousin and I toddled behind them, loving the drama and the attention. When we got to the car, my uncle thanked us all and said we were getting treats. By the time Schumacher hit the accelerator, we were all sitting on the couch eating ice-cream, with the crying cousin – who had performed so well, shedding tears on cue – being rewarded with a Kinder egg as a bonus.

When I realised that my uncle was willing to bend and break the rules to facilitate his love of Sunday-afternoon sports, I temporarily lost all faith in real human adults, and I decided very young to place all of my demands for guidance and formative inspiration onto television.

Most of my childhood consisted of watching television and eating Coco Pops or toast. Or both. I didn't realise it until much later but my attraction to complex carbohydrates started at a young age and meant that I was always referred to as 'a fine big girl'.

We had 'multichannel' in our house, so my mother and uncle could watch the aforementioned grand prix. Not many people in my small hometown had multichannel. I remember my friends only having 'poverty one and poverty two'. I think the Irish-language channel TG4 had already started, but no one had taken the time to tune it in.

There were definitely people in my school who were friends with me only because of my access to extraterrestrial television, but at the time I didn't notice or care. A friend was a friend – and mine got to watch Nickelodeon.

Because of the little black box with the red digits, I had the pleasure of sipping the chocolate milk at the end of my cereal bowl while listening to American accents advertising things to me in dollars, nickels and dimes. For sixty minutes every day after school, from 4:15 to 5:15, before my mother got home from work, Channel 13 broadcast Nickelodeon. It was torturous in its rarity. It was like people in solitary confinement being let out for sixty minutes a day to soak up enough vitamin D to stop them from withering before being thrown back into the darkness. That sixty minutes gave me snippets of exotic

American adolescence, just enough to tantalise me and keep my hopes of escaping provincial Ireland alive.

My mother and I were always on the road. On weekends, we would drive to Cork city. During school holidays, we would go to Dublin or Wexford or Spain. It wasn't until my late teens that I spent any downtime in Mallow. It seemed to me to be a place we were always waiting to get out of, even if only for an afternoon. I never really understood why we ended up in Mallow in the first place. Mam and I moved there from Dublin when we came back from Germany so my mother could work for my uncle who owned a garage and petrol station. Apart from that, there was no link to the town. That's not the case now. Even though I have moved away, my mother still lives there and wouldn't move for all the world, but as a child it seemed like we were always in one of Michael Schumacher's pit stops, just waiting for the guy to lift the barrier so we could speed off to somewhere that sold branded clothing and real Chinese food.

I had my afternoon routine scheduled around my hour of Nickelodeon. I would catch the last fifteen minutes of *Kenan & Kel*, a full thirty minutes of *Saved by the Bell* and then the first fifteen minutes of *The Fresh Prince of Bel-Air*. Then, just like that, mid-Will Smith, it would go dark and I would grieve for fifteen minutes.

I have most certainly been left with some psychological wounds as a result of the daily mid-show abandonment I endured at the hands of multichannel. I blame it for the fact that I now listen to podcasts at 1.5 times the normal speed, so I get to the end more quickly just in case it is somehow taken away from me. I blame it for the habit I have of buying DVDs and CDs because I feel like if I don't have the hard copy in my library, then I cannot guarantee I will be able to watch the whole thing when I want to. Regular scheduled programming on TV or online will never be able to reconvince me of its reliability.

After my Will Smith bereavement had passed, I would pick myself up, brush myself off, refill my cereal bowl and switch to Network 2 for a full episode of *Sabrina the Teenage Witch*.

Everything I needed to know in my youth I learned from that show. I dedicate this whole chapter to Nell Scovell, the creator and writer of the most influential piece of fiction in my life.

Sabrina taught me what mitosis is and algebraic lessons like how to find the slope of a line. More importantly, the show's strong feminist message helped me to accept that my non-nuclear family upbringing did not make me a freak and actually would benefit me in the long run.

Sabrina lived with her two aunts, Zelda and Hilda, and a talking cat named Salem. Her mother would turn into a ball of wax if she ever laid eyes on her, and her father existed only in a book.

I didn't have a dad growing up and because of that show, that became totally normal and OK.

Even though it was about a teenager with magic powers, the running theme was that you can't solve problems with magic and there is no easy way out of life's difficulties. Not everyone liked Sabrina, and that was fine, too. She struggled with the meanness of Libby, the school bully, season after season, only to learn that

Libby's mother is unbearable and poor Libby is just a product of her environment. Before any other TV or film capitalised on the trope, I learned from Sabrina that school bullies like Libby usually have parents who are even worse bullies.

She taught me to take responsibility for my actions. When she got caught riding her vacuum cleaner without a licence, it was lying about it that was the real crime. It's OK to make mistakes, I learned, but it's up to you to make it right again. In another episode, Sabrina split herself into four because she was trying to please four different people. In that episode, I learned that if I do what is right for me with the guidance of other people, I am less likely to develop split personalities.

One episode sticks with me above all others. The show was revolutionary because of its tacit feminism. The actors were mainly female and looked like they actually ate dinner. It was a refreshing contrast against the backdrop of the 1990s rise of catwalk anorexia. In the episode, Sabrina became obsessed with her weight and decided to try out a crash diet, calling up a witch friend to buy a magic pill called Blubber-Be-Gone. The pill actually enchanted the mirror in her bedroom so no matter how much weight she lost, her reflection was growing bigger and bigger. After taking too much Blubber-Be-Gone, she became invisible. Her friends talked about her in the hallways as she stood within earshot, unseen. They talked of how independent and confident she was, all of the things that Sabrina had lost in that episode. This eventually brought her around to a restorative realisation.

'All I needed to restore myself was a little self-esteem, and I definitely don't need to diet,' she said. 'Tonight, I realised that what a person looks like on the outside doesn't matter half as much as what she's like on the inside.' As I sipped on calorific chocolate milk and ruined my appetite for my dinner, which I would still eat anyway, I appreciated the theme of external looks being less important than personality. It wasn't until years later that I would learn that this is an idealistic view that, unfortunately, doesn't always hold up in the real world.

For pre-teen Stefanie, Sabrina and her aunts were the perfect role models. They were imperfect, brash, empowered, smart, compassionate and clumsy. They all made big mistakes, and sometimes were able to fix them but other times had to learn to live with the consequences of their actions. They were always loved and supported, even when they were spiteful or envious or just moody.

My youthful dependence on television led me to believe that I would one day grow up and have all of my ducks in a row. The world I grew up in taught me that I would own a house, have a family and be fully sure of my next steps by the age of twenty-eight at the latest. However, now I feel I live in an alternate universe where the rules are different. I don't get to buy a house, I get to walk around the Monopoly board renting houses from the landlords who pile the little properties too close together and hike the price above market average. There's a different Monopoly rule book that I haven't been given.

It was a gift to have grown up with the sort of influence and role model that Sabrina provided me. It's safe to say that Nell Scovell was my first non-familial mentor and her way of viewing the world shaped me irreversibly. Through her, and indeed my mother and teachers, I learned that there are rules and moral codes in life that keep things on track, but then, of course, you meet the chaos coming at you the wrong way like in an IKEA nightmare and everything starts to change.

2

BIRTHDAYS

AS AN ONLY CHILD, MY BIRTHDAY PARTIES HAD A no-holds-barred quality to them. While other parents had to conserve energy and funds for multiple progeny, my mother had the luxury of unleashing all of her pent-up festivities on one massive annual celebration. And *luxury* isn't a word I use lightly. Keeping it simple was not something we did well.

There were party hats and party games, inflatable castles and, sometimes, an entertainer. There were musical chairs and statues, and the pass-the-parcel prizes were often better than the presents I got from friends. More than once, a parent would become mortified when they picked up their child from my party only to realise they had won a more coveted prize than they had given.

The first birthday I remember was in a house we rented when we first moved to Mallow. It had an empty swimming pool in the back garden and my bedroom was in a turret. The sitting room was split level and the walls were an eerie but elegant shade of turquoise.

My lasting memory of my parties was that my mother was carefree in the extreme. I would be freaking out about people walking Monster Munch into the carpet or spilling ice-cream sprinkles down the side of the couch. I reported everything to my mother and even though she tried to manage my anxiety with casual, nonchalant flippancy, I was eternally concerned that things were right on the edge of chaos. I can still hear her voice in my ear telling me to enjoy my party and play with my friends. That 'it doesn't matter – everything can be cleaned, recovered or replaced'.

When my oldest friend Tom stumbled across the living room floor while trying to catch a frisbee and collided with the television, knocking it off the three-foot split level, we all watched as the black plastic exploded like the birthday piñata we hadn't yet got round to beating. I burst into tears with the stress of the entire day, but my mother quickly set up musical chairs while other adults cordoned off the crime scene to protect us from potential shrapnel injuries. At that point, I wanted everyone to leave. I took my mam aside and asked her how we were going to watch *Gladiators* that night and she said we could watch it in her room and we'd get a new television and it would all be OK. In hindsight, I cherish the fact that she worked so hard – not on my parties, necessarily, but on trying to keep me calm in what she knew was a stressful situation. She knew me before I knew myself. She knew that I wasn't counting the days in excitement but in anticipation. I was counting down in the same way people count down before they jump out of a plane: 'Three, two, one … THERE'S A SMALL CHANCE I WON'T SURVIIIIIIIIIVE.'

My birthday is on April 21. Having survived April Fool's Day unscathed, I would count down the days to my birthday. I always counted in sleeps. We had a credit union calendar hanging in the kitchen and I would come down every morning and count how many sleeps were left. When I had counted and recounted them, I would then bring the figure to my mother for confirmation. 'Is it nineteen sleeps now?'

I had a conspiratorial suspicion that if I didn't check every day, someone might move the date closer or farther away and I would miss my birthday. It was a fear that started during a game of Ludo one summer. A girl I met on holidays rolled the dice and got a six but she moved eight places, skipping over me, getting 'home' first and winning. Fool me once, Samantha from Majorca, fool me once.

I still believe that birthdays are a really important day. It's the one day of the year where you get to individuate from everyone else in your life (unless you're unlucky enough to have to share a birthday) and people gather to celebrate the fact that you are an actual living person. It's like an annual achievement of Maslow's top tier in the hierarchy of needs.

I remember being slightly miffed the first time I met a person who had the same birthday as me. It was such a personal, identifying detail about me and I was raging I had to share it. She was named Jackie and she was a year older than me. I still think of her every year on my birthday, and even though I haven't seen her in probably two decades and I am certain she is a lovely woman, I still harbour a little resentment for the fact that she was the first person who highlighted the reality that I am a common, un-special cog in a massive human-race wheel.

In secondary school, I picked up a book about Taureans – looking for some explanations about why I am both supersensitive and super robust – and I learned that I share my birthday with the Queen. I was filled with pride. It was as if, by sharing my birthday with the head of the royal family, I had been re-gifted the exclusivity I had felt before I met Jackie. But then I realised that the Queen has *three* birthdays and I was raging again.

So my parties always had that throw-everything-at-it feel that had historically been reserved for the dowry of the single daughter on her engagement. In the weeks running up to the Big Day, I would oscillate between being sleepless because of excitement about what cake I would have or what games we would play, and being sleepless in terror at the idea of having other kids in the house who might want to play with my toys. I always ended up crying at my birthday party, sometimes when the kids had gone home but more often when they were there.

Once it was because Katie was going too hard on my blue colouring pencils. Another time, Tom was rearranging my Sylvanians and I just didn't think it was right or proper that the badgers and the frog should share a room in my mansion. It's hard having to share your stuff with ten kids who are high on sugar and free of their parents.

I remember on more than one occasion pulling my mother quietly aside and asking her to please end the party and call all of their mammies and daddies because I'd had enough. She didn't. She couldn't have, really, so she invented a new rule to protect me from the upset of sharing. It quickly became one of my favourite parts of my birthday ritual and I was known to use it outside of birthday season too. It was hiding all of my good toys 'up high' so I wouldn't have to share them or have anyone touch them. Mam had a rule that if people came to the house, I had to share anything they wanted to play with, so if I didn't want people playing with something, I had to hide it and not produce it on the day. I think this was my first lesson in not boasting. I wasn't allowed to show off my cool stuff unless I was willing to share it – and I was rarely willing to share it.

Other children's parties were even more stressful than my own. My friend Seán had a brother named Lorcan, who we were told was allergic to chocolate. We had to hide our chocolate from him, but we also had to let him play with us and not tilt our heads in pity when we met him because, apparently, there was nothing wrong with him and he was 'normal'. I sometimes wonder what became of him. This was a time before children had peanut allergies, so nuts were laid out on the table with the other sweets but, sometime in the late 1990s someone's neighbour's cousin's friend died of a peanut allergy at a birthday party from just the smell and that was the end of the salty snacks.

I never wanted to be picked up first from other people's parties – but not last either. I lived in fear that everyone was waiting for me to be collected from any given party so they could continue without me and start the *real* party. If I wasn't the first to leave, I couldn't be duped.

No limit was put on the number of friends I was allowed to invite to my parties. However, I lied and told a few classmates that my mother was only allowing me to have ten friends there.

As a child, you have very few situations in which you can flex your control-freak muscles, so the chance to be judicious with my invitations was delicious. More delicious, I suspect, than the Bosco birthday cake I had when I was seven. That birthday sticks out the most simply because there are so many photos of it. There were face paints, enough sweets to constitute child abuse and more children than I wanted to be there.

Photos of me with various toys I received each year lie in drawers in my mother's house. The nostalgia bombs go off when I pick up a Smyths catalogue today and see that some of my favourites are being re-released – Stretch Armstrong, Polly Pocket, Sylvanian Families, finger skateboards, crash dummies, Sonic for the Sega and anything with the Teenage Mutant Ninja Turtles on it.

They weren't ninjas when I was young. They were just heroes. But I adored them. I had a bin in the shape of an oil drum that I got as part of a Turtles-themed birthday and it was better than any of the hi-tech gifts I got that year. I mean, Hi-tech like V-tech y'know? Because I would have hidden all the toys I got for each birthday in a bid not to have to share, my parties were less about toy-play and more about horse-play. I recently came across a photo of a friend of mine scaling up a doorframe, another of me precariously balanced on one leg on the edge of a see-saw, another of my cousin smoking my grandfather's pipe. At some point, I must have spilled something or bled onto my outfit because a costume change features. Vomiting from overfeeding is also a possibility.

It's hard to believe that adults just stood around and took photos of us doing these dangerous things. Maybe I've just been bitten by the overly cautious bug and am destined to never let my children outside without double vaccinations, GPS trackers and bubble wrap, but I am vaguely horrified by the young boy framed by the door. His legs and arms are splayed out into the doorframe, his face etched with the effort it is taking but also trying to smile for the camera. This boy is now a world-class jockey. Imagine if he had fallen and done some serious osteo-damage and ruined the bright future that was ahead of him.

This photo stands out because there's a photo very similar to it taken on my eighteenth birthday. In the eighteenth-birthday photo, it is not the jockey who is splayed in the doorframe but a schoolmate so drunk she is using the doorframe to keep herself vertical. Side by side, the photos are glaring proof that birthdays, and how they are celebrated, change dramatically as you age.

I think my seventh birthday was the last 'normal' birthday, if they ever had a stasis because, at aged eight, I was forced to have my first off-site party. My friends and I were too 'cool' for parties in our houses by then. I was the youngest of my group and had endured a year of Happy Eighth Birthday Parties in grungy bowling alleys and sticky cinemas, and had ingested too many birthday chicken nuggets. When April swung around and I turned eight, I said goodbye to the last remnants of a controlled environment by going to THE CIRCUS.

I hated the smell, I hated having to share my birthday with the general public, I hated the fact that there was no biggest slice of cake for me (we all got the same-sized candyfloss) – didn't they know who I was?

I also hated the noise and the crowds and the clowns and the animals, and spent the entire time actively avoiding eye contact with the psychotic circus master who dragged any children who looked at him into the ring to do cartwheels and run away from freelance horses and baby elephants. It was horrific. My friend Chloe made eye contact and was hoisted into the ring to jump from a height onto a crash mat. The photos make it seem like she enjoyed the debacle, but I suspect the clown bewitched the camera with some sort of circus sorcery because there is no way anyone could have enjoyed a single moment of any of it. I sobbed that night after everyone had gone home, and swore I would never have a birthday party or go to the circus again. I have broken both of those commitments.

(In my defence, it was not because I developed a love of 'Carnival' but because I attended the Gaiety School of Acting and they made us do a circus course with Duffy's. It remains my career nadir and that is something I really hope will never change.)

The vow to never celebrate my birthday again had disappeared by the following January when the sheen had worn off my Christmas presents and I'd started craving my next consumerist haul.

The pre-teen and teenage birthdays are a blur of one off-site stressor after another. There was the time we went to see *Beethoven* and, when we came out of the cinema, my mother's car windscreen had shattered because a 'For Sale' sign had fallen on it. There was the time Veronica wet herself at *Blood Brothers* and I had to sit next to her and the smell all the way until the last bar of 'Tell Me It's Not True'. There was the time we went to a pizza place and, even though she didn't say it at the time, when we got to school on Monday Jane claimed she had found a pubic hair in her garlic bread, and somehow it was my fault. By the time I reached eighteen, through the sheer anguish of the birthday parties that had gone before, I was so ready for my first drink.

I didn't drink before my eighteenth birthday – but I made up for it on that night. I sipped so enthusiastically that April evening, and puked with equal gusto the following morning, that I didn't drink again for months. The glass is never half full or half empty if you always drink doubles.

Every teen birthday I remember wanting to be eighteen so badly. And then twenty-one. Now, I scramble away from every birthday like those swimmers trying desperately to climb out of the pool before the performing whale catches them.

Never has something changed so drastically from being looked forward to, and even craved, to being feared and something to be avoided at all costs. The great thing about being over eighteen, aka 'an adult', is that you can plan, organise and host your own parties – or not, if that is what you choose. My recent birthdays have included an even more scaled-down list of VIPs – Valued Interminable Pals – meeting for planned activities in controlled environments. Bet you're jealous you haven't been invited, aren't ya? It's like Monica says in *Friends*, 'Rules help *control* the fun.'

I quit alcohol when I was twenty-five – I'll get to that later – and, since then, I haven't hung out in bars or around drunk people. This means I rarely attend other people's parties but always make an effort to take a friend for lunch on our own for their big day.

My birthdays, then, tend to be food-oriented. Two years ago, I went to Nando's with five friends and had a long lunch over peri-peri wings and left when I was extinguished by all the extroversion. They were five of my closest people, so they understood totally that that was all I was able for, and I was spared the disappointed looks of oh-we're-*leaving*-but-I-got-a-blow-dry-for-this. Last year, I scaled it down even more and dragged my birthday day into a birthday week and met each friend for our own little lunch celebration. That way I got to *actually* engage with each of them ... *and* I got a week's free lunches. Like all the best things in my life, my birthday celebrations are a low-key, no-obligation affair.

Based on the terms and conditions of every bouncing

castle hire company's website that 'the use of bouncing castle equipment by adults and larger teenagers is not permitted and is not covered under insurance', it's not difficult to understand why birthday parties change. It's the clause, 'larger, more boisterous children are kept segregated from smaller ones' that highlighted the real truth to me. Not only do birthdays change – and here's the newsflash – so does your age. One year, you're bouncing on an inflatable castle; the next, you're standing in the corner of the party sipping a soft drink resentfully wondering about where those new hairs under your arms came from.

When I was in school, I was told I could do anything I wanted. Anything. That's a terribly false promise to feed a growing mind.

While I was trying to figure out who I was, I was asked what I wanted to be. And then I was told, 'Money is the sweetest thing. You can have every iPad and diamond ring. You can buy happiness for you and others around you.'

And I saw it.

I saw €50 notes exchanged for T-shirts at concerts. Concerts where we couldn't sing along because there were too many tracks on too many albums and we had every single one but no time to listen. At these concerts, they sold and we bought T-shirts we never wore. T-shirts that hung in a wardrobe, fading, with us outgrowing them. We were chasing the next hit.

Get a twenty, get fifty, get a move on.
You're missing it.
You're too young to work but
there're too many jobs and not enough people.

Steeples in churches full of bells ringing,

choirs singing at Communions that

had become fundraisers.

What name are you taking for your Confirmation?

Britney, Rihanna, Shania.

When I was eleven, I wanted to be a woman.

Have periods. Kiss boys. Have kids. Have a pension.

When I was twelve, I wanted to drive.

A new car.

Every year.

When I was thirteen, I wanted an SSIA.

So I could get a boat.

And these weren't dreams.

These were lists I made

on the first page of every new notebook.

Every new notebook that I only ever got five pages into

before a new one caught my eye.

When I was fourteen, I wanted to be heard.

When I was fifteen, I wanted to disappear.

When I was sixteen, I was asked to seriously consider what job I
    wanted to do for the rest of my life.

I want to work in theatre.

They laughed.

'You're not good enough at English.

And you don't have the looks.

Be realistic.'

That day, I googled liposuction and jaw reduction.

She asked me what I wanted
and then poked holes in it.
Why don't you decide for me?
I did a test.
What career is suited to my personality?
Because I said I didn't like numbers and the outdoors weren't
*   for me,*
they calculated the answers to ten questions and returned
*   unsurprisingly*
with: Advertising Executive with Ebay,
Public Relations Officer with Pfizer,
Hotel Manager of Hilton.
This quiz has been sponsored by various companies.
You don't say.
I went away.
The rest of the day, I sat on the bench outside the church
facing the shops.
Scanning through each of the workers in their shop windows.
Judging.
Because if they didn't own that business, if they only worked
*   there,*
they had a job and not a career.
And that's not the life I was made for.
I was made for great things.
And I sat there, waiting to accept an identity that someone
*   would give me.*
Would they hurry up?

In school, I got picked last for sports.
I wasn't surprised. In shorts,
I looked even worse and my knees
had dimples on them.
They still do.
I wanted to work in theatre.
Why was that so easy to dismiss?
Granted, I never said it with much conviction.
It was always offered apologetically.
Because I'm a woman.
I was made to expect something that didn't come.
Given a bus stop and a timetable, a route planner
full of pit stops to fame and happiness.
A straight road to the top.
But the bus never came.
And I stood there for a while
with puddles splashing me when cars passed.
And people were slow to tell me to walk.
Because they were embarrassed.

I hate the change that comes with every birthday. It's a day where you look back and think, *Where was I this time last year?* And then you start down memory lane, which is a very dark lane with very poor street lights, and everything seems threatening and just out of reach.

It's only half as bad as, *Where will I be this time next year?* The unknown. It gives me the feeling I get when people chew cotton wool. What if I've changed completely? What if I have wrinkles? What if I turn thirty and I still don't have my own house? A mansion? A millionaire husband? A full set of children? A holiday home and a matching toaster/kettle set?

3
HO-HO HOAX

I SAW HIM.

I swear to God, I saw him.

I was ten. We were driving to my aunt's house. We reached the peak of the hill on a dark December evening and, just as we turned the corner, I saw a sleigh disappear into the clouds in the sky. The sleigh was being pulled by reindeer, but I could only see the back four hooves because of the clouds. I now know this is a molecular impossibility, but I swear to you that I saw it. I believe that my childhood self was not lying and that the power of the Santa myth made me see the sleigh in the sky. That is one of the reasons why finding out 'The Truth About Santa' was especially traumatic for twelve-year-old me. Yes. Twelve.

I have asked my friends about this and many of them have said that, from the time they fully understood what Santa was, they were looking for proof that he wasn't real. I was completely the opposite. When I found a box on the top shelf of the storeroom at my mother's work that had 'Stef's Santa Presents' written on it, I completely accepted the lie that Santa had left them there because there were so many that they wouldn't all fit in his sleigh. When one kid told me at a birthday party that Santa wasn't real, I put him in my bedtime prayers that night: 'Dear Jesus Christ, please bless Matthew and make him believe in Santa because he always helps the other boys with their sums so he's definitely on Santa's "good" list. So please can you help him to believe so he has a good Christmas?'

I would still believe in Santa today if Naomi hadn't told me. I am always ready to accept the rules and myths of the world, the things that explain away the mysteries of life. I simply would never have considered the possibility that someone would lie about Santa. Because why would you? My friends all found out before me. I feel a great need to thank them right now for not ruining the magic for me. I was the baby in my group of friends, so maybe the fact that I still believed was keeping Christmas alive for the whole group. The lies that filled the year, or perhaps two, when I still believed and they didn't made it extra hard when I finally did find out. In protecting me from the truth, my friends created elaborate sightings and stories of near misses and bells jingling at night time – to the extent that the last two years of my Santa-believing life were probably the most magical.

One friend called me over in the schoolyard one day. Her parents were getting an extension on the house and part of the construction work involved getting rid of the chimney and replacing it with a wood-burning stove. I would absolutely never have made any connection or spotted any Santa-confirming issues with this because it wasn't my house. My egocentrism is at its most potent during Christmas. My friend saw a potential hole in the lie and took it upon herself to protect me. When she called me over, she opened up her hands to reveal a tiny note which she said had been sent by the elves and delivered to her by one of the builders working on her house. The note said, 'Santa knows your chimney is gone but he'll still bring presents.' I didn't question the fact that it was in her handwriting and written on the fancy paper I had given her, I just bounced next to her in joint excitement at the upcoming delivery of presents. I was just so willing to accept anything that was thrown at me with enough conviction.

I was a clever kid. I was also empathetic. I started to have issues with Santa when I was nine. I believed in him very much, and that was part of the problem. I had a very close friend at the time who lived in a council estate near me. I never noticed any difference in our lives or our parents' means, except at Christmas.

One evening, my neighbour Edel was in babysitting me. I asked her to put my hair into braids like Kel had on the TV show *Kenan & Kel*. Despite the fact that Kel's corn rows were helping him to control his afro, Edel went about plaiting my sleek black hair into a million braids. I've always found it easier to ask big questions when I can't see the face of the person answering me. Maybe it's because I'm happier being lied to and, if they lie to my face, I will know. As she ripped the hairs out of my head in tiny strands, I watched the lametta on the Christmas tree moving, as if by magic, floating in the heat rising from the radiator below it. I thought about my friend from the council estate and I worried about the contrast of contents in our Christmas stockings.

I asked, 'Why do kids who have more money get more presents?'

I remember Edel pausing – she pretended she had dropped a bobble. Eventually, she said, 'They don't. You just think that because they probably get so much that they forget to tell you some of the things when you ask them.'

I had to edit the answer a little in order for my inquisitive mind to accept it. When my friends got their presents it was Christmas Day, we weren't back to school until two weeks after that, so it was completely plausible that some of the presents could have become irrelevant, been eaten or even have broken, and so were no longer worth reporting.

Perhaps it was my steadfast belief in Santa that made me as scared of him as I was excited. I would be lying if I said I didn't have stress nightmares in the run-up to Christmas – basically, every second night after Hallowe'en. The suspense, the surprises and the omnipotent power of the Man in the Red Suit wasn't dissimilar enough to the pervasive cautionary tale of the Man in the White Van for me to sleep easy. I was terrified of Santa. I was also terrified of being terrified, because I felt like if he knew I was terrified, he wouldn't like me and so wouldn't give me presents.

I'm not the only kid who experiences the phenomenon of Santa trauma. Apparently, it's a completely legitimate thing. In my case, I didn't get the complete aversion that sees kids trembling behind piles of Lego after their first trip to Santa's grotto, screaming and running away from any man with a beard. I didn't get the part of the trauma where books and films about Santa frightened me into a thumb-sucking foetal curl on the floor. My fears around Santa came from the traditions around his visit. The lyrics to the songs we sang at school suggested that Santa could see me when I was sleeping, knew when I was awake, was well-equipped to judge me on my behaviour and categorise me thereafter. There was also the Christmas tradition that I learned about in films and on TV of hanging your stocking on the end of your bed for Santa to fill with presents. My stocking was left on the fireplace but that wasn't enough to calm my fear that Santa would come into my room. Maybe he would forget and *think* I was one of the kids who did the bed-knob thing and come in to check.

Thank God I lived in a time before The Elf on the Shelf. What a creepy, threatening, weird concept. As if the idea of Santa spying on you when you are asleep isn't scary enough, kids now have a twenty-four/seven Christmas security camera on them whenever they are in a room that has a ledge.

One year, I wrote a letter to Santa that said something close to:

Dear Santa,

Did you get my last letter? I just wanted to tell you please can you give me no surprises this year and can you please not come in to my room? I will leave my stocking on top of your milk glass so you see it and don't need to come in to my room.

P.S. I am really good.

Stefanie

The idea of a strange old man – who has been watching me for months, gathering information on what I liked and watching me when I sleep – coming in to my room on Christmas Eve meant that I rarely got more than two hours of rest every December 24. In my defence, it is fairly traumatic when you look at it. Though I was never as traumatised at the idea of him being real as I was by the idea of him being fake.

I was eating the nougat half of a Double Decker chocolate bar when Naomi Byrne ruined my childhood. My winter devastation started in summer when I met Naomi on holidays in Spain. Our mothers, both single, connected over the plastic sun loungers and they kept in touch after we returned home. The week before we went back to school, my mam invited them to our house for Sunday lunch.

Naomi was getting me to put blue mascara in her hair. She was eating the crunchy part of the chocolate bar and I was eating the soft part. There was silence in the lead-up to it. I'm not sure what her thought process was, I'm sure she didn't intend to ruin my life, she probably had no idea of the effect her words would have on me.

'You know Santa isn't real, don't you?'

Just like that.

Out of thin air she pulled it.

I dropped the mascara. Some of it went on my My Little Pony duvet cover. I balled my fists by my side and did a mighty foot stamp.

'SANTA IS REAL, NAOMI!'

Without giving her the space to prove it, I demanded she help me wipe the mascara off my bed. We did it together in silence. I actually can't remember speaking a single syllable to Naomi since screaming my belief at her.

When Naomi had left, I bombed down the stairs to confront my mother. I was confronting her in the hope that she would, yet again, confirm that Naomi was just another hopeless case destined for coal and empty stockings.

'Mam, Naomi says Santa isn't real.'

She has since told me that, in the minutes that passed between my statement and her response, she was doing fast maths. My mother quickly calculated the months to Christmas and hazarded that I would be over the trauma, added my age to the possible number of years a child *can* believe and decided to hit me with the truth.

'She's right, Stef. He's not.'

She thought I really wanted to hear the truth? I *never* want to hear the truth. My statement hadn't even been a vague hunch. It was not a question. I was not looking for answers.

'YOU LIED TO ME!'

I sobbed. I sobbed and wailed. Each tear that plunged down

my face carried with it an ounce of innocence I would never get back. A big hole inside me that Santa used to fill had been ripped out of me. In a matter of minutes, I felt all of the horrible things that religious people must feel when internet trolls attack them. It was my first bereavement, my first memorable grief. To my child-ears, it was the same as hearing that Santa's sleigh had been hit by a Boeing 737 and he and all the reindeer were dead, and that was it.

The certainty, the fervour, the audacity with which I had believed the lie made the acceptance of the truth immediately mortifying and shameful. No more deniability. I remembered instantly every time I had ever ardently exclaimed my belief in the man himself. Every letter written in my best cursive, every sleepless night listening for bells on the roof. Every list I rewrote to make it neater and less greedy. Every carrot I peeled for Rudolph. Every glass of milk left in an iced bain-marie to keep it cool.

The sadness that coughed and gagged and snotted out of me was the reality that the whole world was just a tad less delightful, a bit more sinister. The possibilities of the world diminished instantly.

My mother tried to mitigate my heartbreak. She said all of the things that are in the script of The Big Santa Reveal. 'He's real if you believe in him.'

'But you just said he's not!'

Then a pause. More tears flooded out of me as I realised another layer of loss. 'Does he not even bring my stocking presents?'

My mother, without missing a beat, turned away from me to make me hot chocolate and to hide the forthcoming lie, which she said in shock. 'Oh no, no, no. Of *course* he brings your *stocking* presents.'

'Oh. So it's just that you bring my big presents?'

'Exactly.'

'Oh.'

I think it was like when Edel was braiding my hair. I couldn't see her face, and I was happy to accept the lie.

The new lie soothed me until school started. My friends checked in with me around November.

'What are you getting from Santa, Stef?'

'Santa isn't real,' I replied.

And poof!

I was the last person in our school year to find out and, with that one sentence, that one admission of reality, none of us were children anymore.

All I ever wanted was for Brenda Fricker to appear to me in a park, covered in pigeons and teach me the meaning of Christmas. Is that too much to ask?

Most children become aware of the implausibility of Santa over time, gradually, like particles settling onto the bottom of a snow globe. But when I heard the truth, my trust in my mother – and thus in all people and facts – was temporarily called into question. I'm lucky that I never asked my mother outright if Santa was real. She never looked into my eyes and lied to me, so it didn't put the strain on our relationship that it could have.

She still blinks back tears of guilt when she recounts the

day I found out the truth. The perennial parental problem. My mother had done such a good job of making Christmas and the Santa myth real that our trust was temporarily bruised when I found out otherwise. The truth hit me like a snowball in the face. A snowball, thrown by Naomi and not intercepted by my mother.

In the following days, the aftershocks came in the form of constant questioning of every fact she had ever told me. If my mother could lie about this, what else was she hiding?

'So is Jesus a lie too?'

'No, Jesus is real.'

'Prove it.'

'I can't.'

'So, he's not real.'

'No, he is real, but you have to have faith, because there's no proof.'

'No, I don't believe in Jesus until I have proof. What about the tooth fairy?'

'No. You know the tooth fairy and the Easter bunny aren't real.'

We had been through the tooth fairy and Easter bunny debacle years earlier. I never bought the Easter bunny because it was a goddam *rabbit* and I was just not willing to be hoodwinked by anthropomorphism. A man who could circumnavigate the world in a matter of hours while stopping off at every residential property occupied by people of the Christian faith – sure. A bunny who delivers eggs – as if.

'What about Gay Byrne?'

'Gay Byrne?'

'Yes. The toy show man. Is he real?'

'Yes, Stefanie. Gay Byrne is real.'

'Promise?'

'I promise you Gay Byrne is real.'

It was a small win, but it was enough for that year.

The following Christmas, I remember being distinctly jealous of the kids who still believed. But I was even more freaked out than before at the idea of adult men dressing up as Santa and I refused to sit on their laps.

I asked Edel why she had lied to me. She said that it wasn't her place to tell me, and she taught me how to keep the secret alive for other kids. I decided I never wanted to be like Naomi. I never wanted to be the kid who ruined another child's life.

Gradually, I started to appreciate that my mother had spent a significant portion of her income on presents for me, on trips to Santa, decorations, posting letters upon letters to him to alleviate my anxieties, all in the spirit of altruism, never looking for praise or thanks. Maybe *that* is the magic part of Christmas. For once, people do good and actively avoid getting the credit for it.

Nana has the housing alarm system Netwatch. They shout at me over a loudspeaker from somewhere north of Bandon and tell me to step away from the property. They call the phone in the house and in the neighbours' to tell them someone is entering the premises. It's 2 p.m. on a Tuesday, and Nana believes that if you're paying for a twenty-four-hour service, then why *not* leave it armed all day?

Nana gets *The Irish Times* and the *Independent* newspapers delivered to her every day. A man in an Opel Astra drops them to the house between 3 a.m. and 4 a.m. The sound of the letterbox startles me out of sleep every time I stay over, because I think Nana has fallen on her way to the bathroom. Then, sometimes, the phone rings. It's the alarm company calling to tell us that someone has been to the house and driven away. At least five times I have explained to them that it's just the papers and it will continue to happen on a nightly basis until print media dies. They're obviously not taking any risks.

I see these Netwatch posters on the pillars of big houses across the country. Some of these gardens also contain trampolines and brightly coloured swing sets. I wonder how the children in these families broach the threat of Netwatch in their letters to Santa. I see kids who know how to set up websites and order PlayStation games for themselves on Amazon and they never think to google, 'Is Santa real?'

They're just like me. I would never have asked. I had to be told.

When the magic is over, the whole Christmas lark goes downhill for a few years until you turn eighteen and you can legally drink. After that the Magic of Christmas takes on a whole new meaning. Surviving the silly season with your liver intact is the real Christmas miracle. It can also take divine intervention to survive the prolonged exposure to your relatives obligatory in December.

A few traditions have not changed since my childhood. I watch *Home Alone* on December 1 every year. I allow myself a weekly viewing of *Home Alone 1* and *2* until the second week of January. Several times a week, I watch *The Muppet Christmas Carol*, but I don't allow the initial viewing until December 15, and it has to be viewed the first time with the Boy and Girl Housemates. I have no vacancies for any new Christmas movies and refuse to incorporate anything made after 1998. The radio in my car gets tuned to Christmas FM on December 1 and isn't switched back until the airwaves go fuzzy on Christmas Eve at midnight. Similar to the movies, I loathe most new Christmas songs, but I am every marketing manager's dream. If I am exposed to a song enough, I will like it just because it is familiar, so I find myself bopping along to Justin Bieber's Christmas hit in spite of myself. I will never accept 'Stay Another Day' by East 17 as a Christmas song in the same way I do not believe that *Die Hard* is a Christmas movie. Neither is *E.T.*

The first 'legal' Christmas is a real right of passage – at least in my hometown it is, anyway. It's a coming of age that seems increasingly to involve being carried out of nightclubs like the Pietà by boys who only have nicknames. It's a time when all of the progeny of the town return to Mammy from university or farther with their dirty washing. The girls are reunited with the bits of clothing and make-up they had forgotten to take with them and the boys have a freshly ironed shirt for the first time in months.

Myself and the Girl Housemate realised recently that we had both kissed the same boy, on the same night, in the same room, one year apart. Such is the community feel of Mallow, County Cork.

The December Bender was something I did only once. Like any of my life regrets – parachute pants, a bob hairstyle and smoking – I did it because my friends were doing it and I felt I should. In a strange way though, with the December Bender, I'm sort of glad I did it. For no other reason than I now have an eternal comparison for the January Blues. Every January since that one has been a doddle, an un-nauseated walk in the park. When you do the December Bender, January, in its entirety, is a hangover.

The year I did the December Bender, I started it with my college flatmates in Cork city. We did the twelve pubs of Barrack Street on a Monday, 'Christmas Jumper Night' in Redz on Tuesday, someone's house party on Wednesday (the house owner had lit a cinnamon-scented candle to justify calling it a Christmas party) and a Christmas pub quiz on the Thursday. On Friday, pickled in alcohol, we said goodbye to one another and returned to our families for respite. On the Friday night, my old group of pals had planned to exchange Secret Santa presents. Another mandatory night on the town to maintain the streak.

My semi-detached home housed only my mother and me, and was closest to town, so it was inevitable that it would become the 'pre-game' house. My eight friends descended to exchange presents and mascara, banishing my mother upstairs to watch TV or chat on the phone while we got ready for our night out.

GHD hair straighteners were passed around after present pleasantries and suggestive texts were conferred upon and picked apart. Christmas seems to be an acceptable time to rekindle relationships with the people who you spend the rest of the year actively avoiding. The other girls had started their own benders with their college friends back in their university cities, but on our first night together we exchanged presents at night and painkillers in the morning. We left my house at seven and as our bank balances decreased, so did the number of girls in the group. The first to go was tipsy with the disappointment that the present she had received for Secret Santa wasn't as good as the one she'd given. 'I can't believe she actually took the €20 budget rule literally', she slurred loudly into my ear as she put on her jacket and disappeared into the night.

Throughout the rest of the night, my friends fell away one by one. Some actually fell and had to be taken home, some found love with the ghosts of Christmases past and some just got lost in the crowd. The more WKD I downed, the more my head swam with glad tidings for all, and the more I felt connected to my fellow Mallowfornians.

I found an old 'friend' I knew only as Magic. Magic was a sweet boy, maybe two years my junior who kept me in drinks for the entire night. It turns out I get really emotional when I drink mulled wine. Magic and I propped up the bar as he told me about his parents' recent divorce and how his mother was refusing to cook this year and had booked them in to a hotel for three nights over Christmas so she could have a break. I don't know why but I reacted as though Magic was telling me he had lost his home and his family and was sleeping rough outside a bookie's. I sobbed at him and at the injustice. I told him I would bring him home and he could have Christmas with me and my mother and my grandmother. I told him I would send a text right then and there to my mother asking her permission.

I woke up the following morning in the bathroom, red wine everywhere and a message from Manuela, a girl I had been partnered with to do a presentation in Spanish class but didn't know at all. I had spared my mother my drunken text but had instead texted this classmate:

We hat help Majic. 2 turkez slicess it not enoug for him.
It is chris.

I think I meant 'We have to help Magic. 2 turkey slices is not enough for him. It is Christmas.' I have always felt a deep pity for people who spend Christmas Day in a hotel. Being served two pre-cut slices of turkey crown with no brown meat or opportunity for seconds seems like deprivation of the highest order. Worse still is the absence of the glorious nasal statement of mince pies in the oven and the heavy earthiness of a wood fire.

Though a hotel Christmas is not quite as pitiful as the notion of having Christmas on a beach in front of a barbecue. I'm just not sure my adaptability muscles would be able for that.

I vowed never to engage in the December Bender again. The following year, I found myself on a high horse in the same pub, stone-cold sober, raising a glass of Diet Coke to Magic across the bar through thinned lips in the universal expression of hello-but-let's-agree-not-to-speak-to-one-another.

Sober Christmas involved being the 'voluntary' designated driver. For a few years, Coca-Cola had this deal with bars that if you showed them your car keys and could prove you were a designated driver, they would give you free Cokes. Drunk on sugar, I shuttled shit-faced friends to their houses – or worse, the houses of their annual hook-ups – in the back of my immaculate car. I did this for a few years before I had to question my sanity.

I don't meet social obligations like that any more. In fact, I don't really believe in obligations any more. Many of them aren't real to begin with. It's comforting to say on a laboured exhale, 'I *have* to go to her birthday party. She'll be so annoyed if I don't.' That's just your ego trying to make you feel important or wanted. It was so freeing for me when I realised that when you don't go to these things, no one notices or cares. I am not as important to other people as I think I am, and no matter what I do or don't do, the show will go on. I spent long enough giving in to peer pressure. Now, I simply don't do anything I don't want to do.

Certain milestones in your life you can't come back from. About six years ago, my cousin texted me asking, 'Will we not do presents this year?' This is an immovable nail in the coffin of tradition. You never come back from stopping those kinds of rituals. Obviously you can't say, 'No, let's', because they clearly don't want to. If you break the bond and get a present anyway, you will be utterly resented for the gesture and so you have to obey. No one ever sends a text saying, 'Will we start up that costly tradition of getting each other presents neither of us want or can afford again?', and so the habit is broken. The scary part is looking to the future – what happens when we become the oldest generation and have no elderly relatives left? Will the extended family have no place to meet? Maybe that's when the tradition of giving gifts might be crucial – as the only reason you ever see each other ... without that, there may be nothing. Sometimes, the annual unwanted present is the only thing keeping people together.

I put up the decorations with the Boy Housemate most years. We watch *Home Alone* and play Christmas music. It's a strange tradition because I always come across the cards we received the previous year. One year, we came across a card from a guy I had been seeing who had left me before Valentine's Day. The fact that I thought the card worthy of keeping when we took down the decorations in January betrayed the fact that I probably thought he might still be around the following Christmas. He didn't even last until February. Those types of cards go into the bucket next to the fire that is reserved for kindling.

It takes a bit of organising to make sure we are available together to fulfil the tradition. We have to set up the DVD player, make sure we have the obligatory popcorn and hot drinks, we have to get fire logs and scented candles of the right scent ready. We don't *need* to do any of it, of course, but the comfort of tradition is in its consistent repetition.

When I ask the Boy Housemate if he *loves* the tradition as much as I do, he laughs and humours me with a 'Yes of course'. I know he wouldn't be upset if we changed the schedule, but he knows how I love it and so he makes an effort for me. He lies because I don't want to hear the truth that it's just a pleasant frivolity. He knows that, by keeping up the custom and tradition, I am reassuring myself. In the repetition of the old, I am convincing myself that the future will be like the past.

Across the world, we are all complicit in this massive altruistic lie that brings joy to children for a limited time. Maybe if we got rid of the Santa myth and just took credit for the kind things we do at Christmas, the world would be a happier place for more than two days.

The presents don't really matter. Because Christmas with a capital C doesn't matter. And yet it does. Because we have collectively agreed it does. It's an unspoken lie that we all tell ourselves the Christian world over. It's like pretending to be delighted to talk to other people's babies on the phone. It's one of the untellable truths.

It means a lot to my family that I keep Christmas alive. Without me, the only child, the magic is broken. And so I will clap and clap and say, 'I do believe, I do believe', so that the Tinker Bell spell shimmers over our outdoor lights for years to come.

Whether the snow comes or global warming makes it tropical, I will go to bed before my mother, having left out milk that she will not drink. She will lay out the presents she has been gathering since October in a pile by the couch. Each one individually wrapped, the paper bought in the sales the previous January, and she will go to bed. I will set my alarm to wake up earlier than all of the children in the Greenwich Mean Time zone, tip-toe to the sitting room to lay out her presents before she wakes. I will do all of this under the light shed by the Christmas tree lights twinkling onto the shiny surfaces of the room. I will feel briefly guilty that the pile I have for my mother is like Tiny Tim in *The Muppet Christmas Carol* – the sickly, off-colour, smaller version of Kermit the Frog. Then I will remind myself that she is the parent and it's normal that my pile from her would be bigger.

I will lay out the one small parcel for Nana on her chair. Always the same Jo Malone body lotion, each year opened carefully, inspected thoroughly and then commented on with a sigh, 'This one will see me out.' I will have a moment on my own to appreciate just how lucky I am to have my nana and my mother for another peaceful Christmas and then, just as I switch off the lights on the artificial tree, I will pause for an unnoticeable second because I think I might just have heard something on the roof.

For many children, finding out about Santa is a coming of age. You can't unlearn the truth that he isn't real. You can't ignore the new reality that you are forced into. When he is gone, he's gone forever, and no Christmas will ever be the same again. That simple change – Santa going from real to not real – shakes up the rest of your Christmases, and sort of your life, forever. It paints all the holidays that have gone before them with a nostalgic tint you'll never be able to replicate.

Your parents have spent all your life up to that point telling you not to lie and to be good, and then, in one fell swoop, you are introduced to life without free gifts and to the concept of hypocrisy. You're never again going to write a letter to someone addressed only to 'The North Pole' and be sure it'll get there. You will never again make innocent demands of a stranger, blind in the belief and unwavering faith that you will get exactly what you ask for. You will never go to bed with the bouncing excitement that while you are sleeping an ancient magic event is taking place. You grow to realise that Christmas is a consumer-driven holiday that puts parents in debt and the only people who are protected from the stress of the holiday are the ones who are innocent enough to still believe.

As far as I'm concerned, there is no silver lining to the Claus-Con cloud. It's the first rung on the reality ladder that leads to 'and you're going to die, too'. Other rungs include the fact that life is expensive, not everyone thinks you're adorable or will be happy to see you, and that you are majorly going to regret every fashion choice you ever make when you look back on it.

The most sobering of all these reality rungs is that people lie. Full stop. Little lies. Global conspiracies. When you realise you've been conned, all is changed, changed utterly.

Losing the innocent idealism of youth is a massive, earth-shattering change. A massive, earth-shattering, universal and unavoidable change.

4

TILL RENT DO US PART

I MOVED OUT OF HOME AT 6 P.M. ON THE FIRST
Sunday in October 2005. The threat of the move had hung in
the air all day, along with the smell of the Sunday roast. Weaving
its way into the fibres of the new bedsheets and new pyjamas
packed in Tesco 'Bags for Life' under the hall table, just far
enough away from the front door to be unthreatening but not
far enough to pull out.

The hall table housed the landline that hadn't rung in years,
several unopened bills in white envelopes and a few brown ones.

Always open the brown ones, especially if they have a harp on them – one of the pervasive lessons of my youth.

My Leaving Cert results had been dumped on the table a few weeks earlier and were still there. On the day, I got 505 points. I was thrilled with the points but devastated with the results – does that make any sense? 505 was a figure I felt reflected the work I had put in, but I only got a B2 in English and then got this completely unexpected A1 in Biology. So the points were there, but I felt I had let my English teacher down completely and was too much of an illiterate dunce to be starting my Drama and Theatre Studies degree with just a B2 in English when I had predicted an A.

I obviously still have some trauma about that grade because I still feel the need to clarify for you that I came up ten points in English in a recheck, OK?

With my 505 points I was well above the 375* I needed for my course. The asterisk meant that I had to audition to get into the course as well as make up the points. I spent hours practising my monologue in front of drama teachers, industry professionals and mirrors but, because it was Shakespeare, I convinced myself (and my education-focused mother) that it could be classified as 'revision'. Seventeen-year-old Stefanie had no sense of how talent casting works. It would have been a strategic move for me to look at myself from someone else's perspective and realise that no casting director who valued their reputation was ever going to call me to read for Juliet. But that didn't stop me.

Baz Luhrmann had presented me with a Juliet I easily

identified with. Claire Danes' hammy melodramatic excesses made me feel like my own hormonal mania was some shade of normal. And we both look really weird when we cry. I watched her balcony scene with Leo over and over, practising each beat and working myself up to tears when I was forced to say goodnight to this boy I had just met and whom I had just organised to see tomorrow. (Note to self: Can you sue films for calcifying underlying abandonment issues?)

I do feel lucky now, however, to have had a film to watch about teenage love that didn't include vampires.

The audition went well, the exams ditto, and the results and points came in. I survived the debs and now all that was left was to move out.

I hadn't wanted to go to my debs. I had organised with my friend that we would go together but, at the last minute, he dumped me and accepted an invitation from a mutual friend of ours. My mother made me go. My gay friend Tom stepped in as Prince Charming and brought me to the ball. I tolerated it until it was an acceptable time to call my mother to come and pick me up.

I was asked by my classmates to give a speech to wrap up our schooldays, possibly because people who weren't me thought that I was the funniest one in the class or possibly because the girls knew that if I wasn't given a job, there was a chance I wouldn't show up out of social anxiety. I hadn't yet realised that you can say no to invitations, so I made the most of it when I was there – no one likes a sulk.

As I prepared to leave home to start university, I thought that if I could survive the mass gathering of thin girls in beautiful gowns telling me that my hair was lovely and I had 'beautiful eyes', I could survive college, couldn't I?

But I was petrified.

My house was so safe and familiar. I knew what each of the random ticks that went off in the kitchen throughout the day was. I knew which steps on the stairs creaked. I knew that you had to push my bedroom door in before you pulled on the handle to open it or it would stick. I knew that if I put the heating on constant, I needed to put my phone charger next to the timer so I wouldn't go to bed without remembering to turn it off – I never went to bed without my charger. I knew all the ways the house worked and now I was going to be leaving forever.

I was so scared to leave the little nest my mother and I had been living in for fourteen years that I sort of wished she had gone full Capulet and banned me from ever leaving.

But she didn't.

She knew it was time for me to go. I was crossing a threshold. When I left, I would never live at home full-time again. It would change forever. So the night I was leaving, I reckoned forever could spare a minute – or sixty – so I dragged it out until it was pitch dark outside.

I cried when I left the house and drove away on that Sunday night. I let the tears run down my face and neck and soak my collar. My mother would have noticed me raising my hand to my face. She was standing at the door, also crying, and the cars on our busy road wouldn't let me out so I was stuck in this purgatorial hell for at least three minutes, waiting for the traffic to facilitate my coming of age. Eventually, someone let me out and I loved them and hated them for it in equal measure. Juliet's words rolling around in my head.

'Good night, good night! Parting is such sweet sorrow.'

I reversed out the driveway. From that moment onwards, when I referred to 'home' people would ask me to clarify where I meant. 'College home or Mallow home?', 'Dublin or Cork?', and now, after ten years, 'Your home or your mam's?' I left in reverse, moving backwards, like a baby born breech. It's more painful that way.

The night I moved out was the night before I started university. I left it until the last possible minute to go and, even though I was moving only twenty-five minutes up the road, I felt those last fibres of umbilical attachment tear away.

I drove myself and my friend up to the student house we were going to share with six other people. The drive up was tedious and brief. My friend was excited enough for both of us. She had even burned a CD for the drive. There were only seven songs on it, and we didn't ever get around to 'Candy Shop' by 50 Cent featuring Olivia, whoever she is.

I still have the CD and I always skip that song because it doesn't carry the weight that the rest do. The weight given to them on the N20. 'Lonely' by Akon and 'Numb/Encore' by Linkin Park blared out of my Toyota Yaris as my friend bounced her knee eager to arrive. She had half a face of make-up on already, and I knew that meant that she would be club-ready at the first hint of an invitation. I tried to make plans for the evening with her. 'Will we get pizza? Will we watch *Scrubs*?'

Her vague commitment betrayed the fact that she was hoping to land a plethora of party housemates who needed 'connecting with' over cocktails as soon as possible. My stomach tied itself into a knot in time to Daniel Powter's 'Bad Day'. I agree, it was a terrible mix of songs – but that was 2005 for you.

We arrived at the house. It was in a 'student village' close to the university. 'Student villages' are strange places. Not natural, in the same way a zoo is not natural. To have upwards of 200 people who are living independently for the first time all thrown together and to then expect that the fire alarms won't be going off from 1 a.m. to 6 a.m. every night is highly idealistic. In Brookfield, I think we could have benefited from a few chaperones to explain to us how the hob worked, that your laundry doesn't get done magically, and if you leave your plate in the sink, it will still be there when you leave in May if you don't wash it yourself.

My friend and I had seen the house before and her dad had even driven up the previous week and dropped off a small portable television for her room. I followed suit but had mine in the back of the Yaris, the bunny-ear aerial poking me in the back of the head when I slouched, like some overbearing etiquette teacher.

The house, and my room, was ... rustic ... simple ... When my mother saw it, I think she told herself it was fit for purpose.

The interior walls were concrete blocks that had been painted yellow several years earlier. The yellow paint had gathered in the porous holes of the concrete but nothing could give the illusion that this wasn't just painted bare brick. My room had these bricks too, and a single bed built into the wall, a plastic mattress, two drawers under the bed, a chair at a built-in desk, a sink with a fluorescent bulb above the mirror, a wardrobe and a heater. The chair looked like the newest thing in the room, either because no one studied at the desk ever or because so much study was done that the previous chair had had to be replaced. I doubted the latter. One curtain hung over a large square window, which opened only four inches to protect the village from lawsuits.

When we arrived, we got straight down to unpacking. I was finished first and went to my friend's room. She had already made friends. Eight people would be living in the house, including me and my friend. On this first night, only three of the others had arrived. Two boys from Kilkenny – Cian and Ethan – and Amelia from Waterford. Within ten minutes, we had discovered that Amelia and I had mutual friends and that her sister was taught drama by a woman I had been taught by for five months when I was eleven. The two boys hadn't known they were going to be living together but were from the same town and had the same ex-girlfriend. It was just such an Irish introduction to university life.

Cian looked like Worzel Gummidge and Ethan looked like Stretch, the lanky ghost from the film *Casper*. I gave myself these fiction tags to attach to the boys when I realised they were planning a night out and I was certain I'd lose them and not recognise them later on. Luckily, our tolerance for alcohol was not as robust as their enthusiasm to go clubbing because after playing a drinking game with a deck of cards and drinking the vodka someone's uncle had gifted them from Poland, we were all too ossified to step out of the house. Cian had obviously decided that he was going to 'score' on his first night but after chancing the two girls in the house who weren't me, he was pulled aside by Ethan and told that 'you don't shit on your own doorstep'. Cian learned the lesson and made sure to always 'shit' on other people's doorsteps from then on, making his way systematically through the women of Brookfield holiday village for the next eight months.

We may have been too drunk to head out to a club but that didn't save me from the crippling hangover I faced the following morning. When I woke up on my plastic mattress, the ambient scent suggested I was living in an ashtray. My mouth tasted like what I imagine a bag of vacuum-cleaner dust tastes like – dry, dusty, stale with tiny pieces of unknown food stuck to the sides. I got up quickly, determined not to become a lazy student stereotype, and texted my boss at the youth theatre where I had been working at the weekends since I was sixteen years old. I asked him if I could take the Wednesday evening drama class with him as his assistant. I waited impatiently for him to respond, not realising it was only 7 a.m.

I went back up to the scene of the crime. Oh, yeah, for some mental reason our kitchen was upstairs, which was very distressing because it completely went against normality and standard practice. I think it was so the two apartments could have one kitchen on top of the other and that way they saved money on piping or something.

I opened the kitchen door and saw the carnage inside. Then, I made the stupid mistake of cleaning it up. In that simple generous gesture, I cast myself in a role I would never get out of. Like Michael Cera wondering why he is never allowed to be anything other than the loveable geek or Jennifer Aniston screaming to be viewed as more than just a hopeless romantic, I spent the next year struggling against the shackles of the kitchen sink, wondering why no one else ever even offered and empathising too much with Cinderella, scrubbing and sweeping while everyone else went to the ball.

It's hard to individuate from your family when the peer group you are lumped in to live with are all so different from you. The other three girls arrived eventually. Diana and Sarah were from opposite sides of the country but because they arrived together, my brain would never update the information that they had not been friends since school. The other girl was Bríd, I think. All I remember about her is that she was going to study Law and German and seemed very serious. She lived with us for two nights and then she was gone. She didn't say goodbye to anyone. We thought she was in her room for three weeks until, one night, we were all staying in and playing poker and drinking, and our mischievous, conspiratorial minds lost the run of themselves. Ethan and Cian decided they needed to check that she wasn't dead in her bed or something. After googling 'Is there a special victims unit in Ireland?', they took it upon themselves to investigate.

Out the back of the house, they stood on the gravel that, at this point, consisted mainly of cigarette butts from people in the surrounding rooms realising there were no parents around to stop them smoking their brains out. Worzel climbed onto

Stretch, who held him by the ankles. Worzel hoisted himself onto the sill making sure to check if he was drawing the crowd he wanted and, when he was satisfied enough people were watching, turned to announce that the room was empty before jumping off the windowsill onto the grass in a testosterone and beer-fuelled act of idiocy. Girls clapped and he went to chat to the most beautiful of them. That was how we learned that Bríd had fallen at the first hurdle of university.

I like to think she got a second-round place in a course she preferred and not that she felt isolated or sad living with us. I didn't make much of an effort with her, and I always felt sort of guilty about that. I was too wrapped up in keeping myself in university to mind someone else.

When I was at a lecture or at home with my housemates, I was OK. I loved the idea of us drinking and playing cards while eating pizza. But when the idea of having strangers over or, worse, going out to a club was suggested, my anxiety would kick in. Spare me from variables. I would often go back home to Mallow if I knew there was going to be a party in my house.

I tried, but I realised early in the first semester that I couldn't relate to the impulses of my housemates. I didn't want to go out drinking. I was overweight, self-conscious, one-of-the-lads. I saw no enjoyment in putting on uncomfortable shoes and walking into town to pay extortionate amounts of money for drinks that made me sick. When I did go out, I just ran out the clock until people were ready to accompany me to get kebabs and chips. As I watched my friend and my housemates getting off with other attractive drunk young people wearing large green stickers at a Traffic Light Event, I nearly called it a day several times. But I hung on for the post-club chips.

When we entered the club, we had each been offered a sticker: red for 'in a relationship' or 'don't come near me', orange for 'it's complicated but try me', and green for 'gagging for it'. I opted for the red to spare myself the embarrassment of choosing green and not being approached by anyone. That sticker was the university version of the elementary school cop-out of I-have-a-boyfriend-but-you-don't-know-him-because-he-goes-to-another-school. I sipped a drink at the bar and chatted to a shy computer science student who tried to explain the rules of the GAA to me over the bass of 'Don't Cha' by The Pussycat Dolls. Finally, I saw my friend check her phone for the time. The universal signal for I'd-better-leave-now-before-the-queue-at-the-chipper-is-too-long. The friend I lived with ate very little during the day but, after a few drinks, her appetite grew and we would steam up the back windows of taxis with delicious salt and vinegar. For as long as the batter burger lasted, the night had been worth it.

After trying my hand at it and enduring an entire freshers' week, I came to the realisation that student nightlife was not for me. Where does that leave a university student in their first semester? How was I meant to get through the next two and a half years?

This is the big change that struck me from this period in my life. It was the first time I had to choose who I wanted to be. As a kid, identities are thrust upon you. You are a student when the bell rings and until you take off your uniform to change into your leotard, then you're a gymnast until your mother picks you up to bring you to the pool where you become a swimmer for forty-five minutes. You're a grandchild when you're hanging out with your nana and a prize brat when you're exposed to a substitute teacher.

University was the first time there was no one to tell me who to be and, initially, I was completely lost. I didn't know what food I liked to cook, what way I liked my coffee, whether I was the type of person who had breakfast when they woke up or if I wanted to have it a little later in the day. Suddenly, I had options and the agony of choice has sent many before me into a full-on identity crisis. Up to that point, my mother had always encouraged me, with a gentle force, to participate in the milestones of adolescence. I didn't want to go to my Junior Certificate results party, but she made me go. The same thing happened with my graduation party, several eighteenth birthday parties and two music concerts. There comes a point in your life when this changes, when you have the chance to start to individuate and start to find your own end to the sentence 'I'm the kind of person who …'

I sat on the sidelines and watched the social events fly by. From the Law Ball to the themed nights out. It became a source of entertainment for me (and whichever friend was too hungover to go out that night) to drive around and watch the dressed-up students climb into their modified pumpkins and head off to their ball. Until their fairy godmother – in the form of an empty bank account – called them back home before midnight. The themed nights out were always brilliant, and I would get genuinely excited when the posters would go up on campus, in anticipation of the outrageous costumes I was going to witness that coming Thursday. Some personal favourites that stand out were Dungeons and Drag Queens, Dress as a Beatles Song, and Bros 'N' Hoes – even the Literary Society pitched in with their version of a themed party, Tequila Mockingbird. I realised quickly that as soon as I stopped pressuring myself to take part, I could vicariously enjoy the fun.

Daytime student life was more manageable. I would bump into other girls I went to school with as they popped in to our on-campus café to get a quick coffee on their walk between lectures. It was difficult to start bonding at that point because the only thing we had in common was the fact that we happened to choose to attend the same university and we both felt 11 a.m. would be a good time to get a cappuccino. We just said hi at the sugar and milk station and walked on. As I poured sachets of sugar into the froth and watched it sit on top before it sank into whatever small amount of coffee was in there, I wondered if all my actual friends, in other universities in other cities in Ireland, were settling in better than I was. Was I the only one who wasn't getting what was promised when people had said, 'Just get through the Leaving Cert – you will *love* college. It's so much fun'?

My boss did eventually text me back that first morning in the house, after the party. In the afternoon, as I sat with my hungover friend eating pepperoni and sweetcorn pizza in her bed, my phone lit up. He said he would love me to assist him and he would drive us both down to Mallow and back each

Wednesday for the class. The relief ran through my body and made the sweetcorn taste even sweeter.

As I've said, I was heavily influenced by American TV growing up. So when I left Mallow on that first Sunday night and drove the twenty-five minutes to Cork city, I imagined not returning until Thanksgiving or Spring Break or some other holiday we don't even celebrate in Ireland. I never suspected I'd be back home by Wednesday but, two evenings later, we hit the roundabouts outside the city and my heart rate calmed. Living in Cork city was like existing at a higher altitude and not being able to breathe properly. When we hit that weird sculpture of the two naked men on the bareback horses that welcomes you to my hometown, the white faded from my knuckles and I relaxed. I belonged in Mallow, I knew my place. I knew how people saw me and who I was and how to relate to each part of it.

When that changed, I felt completely lost. The liminality, the lack of identity – I just felt so soft and small when stripped of my provincial roots. It was enough for me to drive through the roundabouts on a Wednesday evening. To see the Christmas lights go up in stages, so that I didn't arrive home one Friday evening and see it all changed. I saw all the stages of change. I witnessed each shop close and go dark and then be repainted and refitted and eventually reopened. I didn't have to deal with the trauma of being confronted with the sudden change of the shop name Rings 'n' Things to Karizma.

The young people in the Wednesday drama class were thrilled to see me. Many of them had hopes of becoming professional actors or directors and looked to me and my boss for vocational training. I hadn't realised that by studying Drama and Theatre Studies at university, I was living, relatable proof for them that a career in the arts was not an impossible and pointless pursuit. When the class ended, we sat back into the car and my boss hit the road. I felt the old tug from my mother's house.

'Stop the car.'

'Are you OK?'

'Yeah, is there any chance you can drop me to Mam's? She's working in Cork tomorrow so I'll just go back with her then.'

'Sure.'

He dropped me back to my mother's house at 9 p.m. that Wednesday night. She was thrilled to see me and was somehow prepared for the eventuality that I would just drop in unannounced because she had queen cakes freshly made. Looking back at it, I think she may have turned to baking to fill the empty nest. We never mentioned the fact that I had come running home, we just sat, eating buns, knowing I would go back to my house tomorrow. But tonight, I was home.

In the monologue I did to get into university, Juliet finishes with a couplet. The first line talks about how parting is such sweet sorrow. The second line of that couplet and the resolution of the whole thing is, 'That I shall say good night till it be morrow.'

I never expected that I would take the quotation so literally. I moved out on a Sunday night. I was back in my mother's house the following Wednesday. Baby steps, right?

5

WHY CAN'T PEOPLE JUST STAY THE SAME?

WE ALL HAVE BIRTHDAYS, WE ALL KNOW HOW TIME works, we all know that people age, and we all know that, at a certain age, we die. I know intellectually that the older people close to me are going to die. I know it. But I can't accept it. I *won't* accept it. Even when it happens, when I am standing at their graves, I will be standing in disbelief. It will hit me like one of those dash-cam videos of a train derailing and ploughing into a passing van.

I visit my nana several times a week and I stay with her often. She lives a ten-minute drive away from my house and I have never lived in a world where she isn't right there. I have spent a large portion of every school holiday with her. She taught me how to make sandcastles, how to change a gas cylinder, how to tell the sweet strawberries from the sour ones, how to play *Countdown*, how to do a cryptic crossword, how to play bingo, how to cook a lobster, how to cheat at cards and, most importantly, that mayonnaise belongs in the fridge. She has always been there, sitting in the corner in her chair, smelling of L'Oréal Elnett.

As I type this, she is eighty-nine. I know what the future holds. But I just don't want to live in a world where she isn't right there. She's the centre of the web that connects our whole family. She's the sieve through which news gets disseminated to various relatives – the harder bits reworded to make them more palatable, depending on who she's speaking to. I just think the world will be slightly less well off for not having her in it anymore. She's tried to teach me at least fifteen times, but I can't get my chicken stew to taste like hers. And no one else in the world is so keen for me to 'buy myself something' with a swift placement of a banknote in my hand.

She sits in that chair in the corner of the room, my nana. The same place she's always been. The chair has changed. Now it's electronic. Muscle impulses replaced by electronics to get her to a standing position. Her fingers that once filled patient prescriptions in her chemist's shop now fumble to count out her daily dose. One brown one, one green one, two whites and a cream one. That's all before she gets up. Then there's the white calcium one, which she has to chew and hates. Two brown ones when the Angelus bell tolls at 6 o'clock. Those two are to thin her blood to avoid another stroke. One stroke equals two warfarin. Sometimes one. Depending. At night there's half a sleeping tablet and a white one for cholesterol. She always reminds me that her cholesterol is low, only three point something, but these tablets 'are something to do with strokes too, they've other uses'. She dutifully counts out nine and a half tablets. Sometimes eight. Depending.

Those fingers now curl around a walking stick like ivy growing around a tree, attached to it for support, growing symbiotically closer to it every day.

She goes through her days measuring out her progress by how many times she can walk to the kitchen before withering, how many tasks have been moved onto the 'While I have you ...' list. Dependence on other people to do simpler and simpler tasks, and, although they mean well ... someone keeps leaving the mayonnaise out of the fridge. 'Is it trying to kill me you are?'

She took me to bingo and toy shops and merry-go-rounds. I take her to cardiologists and optometrists and, sometimes, haematologists, depending. She lists off the name and dose of each of the tablets, always intrigued when a new one that wasn't around in her day pops up. They want to measure her height. She tells them what she is. They smile politely. One assures her that he believes she was *once* that height and then he shows her the measurement. She's shrinking. Growing downward, the peak of her life past her and now moving slowly, inexorably towards the ground. She thanks him for the home truth. Writing cheques for checks that all say the same thing: you're hanging in there. Payment for the reassurance that – in their expert opinion – she won't die of whatever *they* are responsible for in the next few weeks. But, sure, 'ring Reception if anything changes'. Fifteen minutes in and out, and four more in the waiting room, all terrified for their news, but drowning it out with daytime TV.

And so we travel home in a taxi, because 'it's easier with the parking spaces and they've the bus lane'. We 'take it easy now' for the afternoon. We sit together and watch home-grown talent on terrestrial stations. The Irish chat show educates me, yet again, as to the various things you can inflict on a salmon fillet. We switch over to 'The English' then at five and do a quiz show or the news. Depending. The quiz shows are the reassuring part because even as I age and gather more general knowledge around me as protection from the world, I still can't beat her on these questions. I chase and I chase, but I'll never catch her. Sometimes, I wonder if I will ever contain all of the knowledge she has. 'Ursine' means 'bear-like' and there are two constellations named after bears, Ursa Major and Ursa Minor. 'Ur-Sa, Ur-Sa,' she says, articulating the Latin word in the hope that it transfers to me and sticks. I'm smiling now as I type, because it has, evidently.

I wish there was a way I could keep her, but time is ticking and the way hasn't been invented yet. Can't I just plug her into something and download her? Can I back her up to the cloud and know that I can bring her back at any time, like my old CVs and university essays on *Don Quixote*? Restore from Backup.

She's happy with her large-buttoned landline and her basic understanding of the iPad (stress on the 'Pad' and not the 'i'). Her iPad has a prayer to St Francis Sellotaped onto the back of it. Memorial cards get Sellotaped on to any surface that will have them. Always either St Francis or a memorial card. Depending.

I wonder if, when I'm old, I'll go back to God. It seems like a very comforting refuge. It's like booking a taxi when the train is pulling into the train station so you don't have to wait in line in the cold. It's like telling your relatives to meet you at Departures and not Arrivals because you can stop the car briefly and you don't have to pay for parking then. Religion may be reassuring to the living, but it's definitely reassuring to the dying.

I just need to start accepting that she'll get backed up to the cloud in a few more years, maybe less. Depending.

6

WHAT WOULD NICOLE SCHERZINGER DO?

AS AN ADULT, I HAVE SO MANY QUESTIONS.

What is a pension? Do I need one? If so, how do I get one? If you tell me to save €50 per week, I'm going to laugh right into your face and then cry because I base my meals around the yellow stickers in Tesco (or Marks & Spencer if I'm feeling flush for cash). Even if I do get a pension, can you guarantee me it will be there when I need it? According to sensationalist news, no you can't.

What is the value of marriage? Should I get married? Like, for tax or something? I would sooner marry someone than get their name tattooed on my body. The latter seems far more permanent and irreversible than the former. I grew up during a time when people were having two, three, four marriages, and it was no biggie. Ross Geller from *Friends* taught me the impermanence of a wedding ring.

What about a credit rating? Is that only a thing in America or do I need one? Will I never get a mortgage because I opened a bank account in college when they tempted me with free Pot Noodles and a bendy ruler and never deposited anything into it?

Health insurance? I've heard that if I don't sign up before I'm thirty-five, I get some sort of disease called 'loading' as a punishment. Can some teacher for adults tell me honestly if health insurance is really and truly necessary when we have public health care in Ireland? I've heard that insurance salesmen are cowboys, but maybe health insurance isn't the same as protecting your iPhone from falling into the toilet. If I spend a massive percentage of my income on health insurance, am I actually covered against all types of things? Can it stop me getting sick? Does it acknowledge the fact that I don't like taking tablets and would prefer a less drug-heavy approach to wellness?

Yes. I am asking if health insurance will cover my gym membership, apple cider vinegar and lentils. Does it cover the other therapies – holistic, physio, occupational, retail? Should I go for the Bronze, Silver or Gold option? And what about my teeth? If I don't get health insurance, am I going to be found rotting in a trolley in the Liffey at low tide and if I do get insurance will I be found begging on side of the canal because I'm so broke?

When you're a kid, there's no pressure on you to deal with any of this. I didn't make my first doctor's appointment until I was twenty-one. I know you may say that I was too sheltered and am now incompetent because I'm inexperienced. I probably wouldn't argue with you. I'm not sure there is an exact threshold you cross when all those responsibilities change, but somewhere between eighteen and twenty-two, the deeds of my life somehow changed hands from my mother's to mine, and it took me quite some time to get a grip of it.

Being an adult is not made easier by the fact that 80 per cent of the things I learned at school are utterly useless to me now. It's great to know that the journey from Dublin to Galway to Cork and back to Dublin is the shape of a scalene triangle, but it'd be nice to know how much it would cost in diesel or what to do if my car breaks down and I'm thirty kilometres from Barack Obama Plaza. I didn't even meet a kilometre during my time at school. Me and miles were great friends and then I left school and all my imperial vices were stripped from me. How often have you used the Pythagorean theorem? Does it make you feel secure for your future that you know how to find the slope of a line? Knowing the Chinese Yellow Emperor died in 2598 BC doesn't stop the anxiety I get when I think about never being able to own my own home.

I appreciate the great teachers I had for imparting wisdom

and guidance and a sense of self to me. I appreciate the shit ones for teaching me that not all people are nice and that primary-school teacherdom is the tiniest amount of power that can go to someone's head. I just wish the things I struggle with on a daily basis, the things that make adult life so hard, had been touched on even a little in school.

When I come up against something I am ill-equipped to answer, I ask myself how someone else would react in that situation. The name of the person and the verb are interchangeable. For instance, if I am going to a photoshoot, I will often have a conversation with the Boy Housemate, sometimes over text, and it will say, 'WWNSW'. This stands for, 'What Would Nicole Scherzinger Wear?' Then, as I look into my IKEA wardrobe of high-street clothing, I find the thing that is closest to what I imagine she might choose and I wear that.

If, on the other hand, I am faced with a difficult producer or tension at work, a situation that requires grown-up decision making, I will either ask my agents, who have become indispensable mentors, *or* I will try to channel strength, dignity, patience and decorum by asking myself, 'What Would Mary Robinson Do?' That woman is an inspiration and I was *so* upset as a child to realise that being the President of Ireland was not permanent like being the Queen. Mary Robinson was the president from when I was two. When I was nine and I realised that someone else had to take over, I was gutted. I just thought that she was the Irish Queen. In my naiveté, I thought that being president was a birthright and she would reign benevolently over our nation until she died and we would all be safe and happy. We haven't had any despots yet, thank God, but Mary is definitely an idol of mine.

In school, no one told us anything about how to navigate an adult relationship. The nuns told us not to have sex before marriage, and we won't get into that. I can't remember what age I was when I got my first period. I wasn't waiting for it, I know that much. I hadn't been aware of periods at all really, and when it decided to arrive – and it wasn't blue water being poured delicately out of a test tube onto a sanitary towel like on the TV – I nearly lost my life. I thought I was dying. I blame my mother and the school for that. I guess each of them thought the other had it covered. I don't remember where I was when I got it either. I think the whole thing traumatised me so much that my young brain worked to erase it from my memory. It succeeded.

I do remember the first time my amateur career as a competitive swimmer collided with my menstrual cycle. I was a competitive swimmer from the age of eleven to fifteen. I was in a swimming club in Mallow, which doubled as a social outlet and the only place I got to hang out with boys. Some of my dearest friendships were doused in chlorine. We trained up to five times a week and all of our spare time was spent in the pool, blocking the swimming lanes and intimidating people who wanted to relax or swim for leisure by speeding past them and doing tumble turns.

I also made my first true boy friend in swimming club. Until I was thirteen, all the boys in my life, outside of cousins, had been sons of friends of my mother or people you happened to be in a kids' club with on holiday. 'Killer', as he was so nicknamed, was my first boy friend as a teenager; I connected with him after we had both sized each other up and found we met a new, teenage set of friendship criteria. Killer was funny, brazen and loved to cause trouble. I watched him antagonise people and then speed off like a fish through the water leaving a trail of bubbles and drama in his wake. We bonded over studying for the Junior Cert exams. He was academically ambitious and that wasn't always something a teenage boy could easily admit without being labelled a nerd. Killer wasn't a nerd, he was athletic and what Americans might call a 'jock' – popular, handsome and adorably unaware of the female attention being scribbled on the walls of convent-school bathrooms.

Although there was never a hope for us romantically, I was really proud, potentially a bit smug, to be able to tell my friends in school, 'Yeah, I know Killer. We're friends.' Of course, this always led to me having to text him and ask him to shift every girl in my year who asked, but he was cool with that, too.

Swimming is an individual sport. You win and lose on your own at the swimming galas. Our club was particularly good at being a community of swimmers, so you never felt the full devastation of not swimming well in a race. Most of the girls in my club were also in my school, though not necessarily in my year. I loved that the team-sport ethos of our club managed to erode the strong barriers that secondary school seems to put up. It was almost unheard of for second years to hang out with first years but, because we were swimmers, we played by our own rules and I spent many a happy lunch-time in the first-year block when I was in second and even third year. I was also elevated to social demigod status in third year when the older swimmers from fifth year would come down to our classroom to chat to me.

But back to my period.

I had a swimming gala I had been training for for months – 6 a.m. starts with coaches blowing whistles and trying to shave 0.03 seconds off each length. Gathering milliseconds together by shaving hair off your body and wearing tighter swimming togs, all in the hope that you would come in less than a second quicker than you did last time. I had worked for months and was on track to race against myself – my old personal best time – and come in faster. And then my 'yolks' arrived. My 'aunt flow', my 'doo-dahs' – or any other creepy, infantilised name Catholic Ireland wants to give them. I was bloated and sore and, looking back, there was no way I was going to be able to race at my best. There's nothing streamlined or technically efficient about a bloated uterus. The issue came long before I was up on the block waiting for the whistle. The issue came when I was presented with my first tampon.

In the changing room of the swimming pool in Nenagh, County Tipperary, I texted my friend who was standing right next to me, so I wouldn't have to deal with the shame of having to say the p-word: 'u hav period gear?' She was older than me, and much more discreet. She plunged both of her hands into her gear bag, wrapped her spare latex swimming hat around the small bullet and then handed me the hat. She walked off to swim her race. I went to the toilet.

Sitting on the toilet, still in my togs, I considered the white bullet. What the fuck was I meant to do with it? I didn't know that there even were ones with applicators but this thing definitely seemed to me to be missing a piece. I used my common sense and tried to insert it. It took a few attempts but, eventually, it stayed there with no support from me. I have never known discomfort like it. I know now that I hadn't inserted it correctly and that's why I couldn't sit down for the rest of the day without feeling like I was being stabbed. I couldn't stand on the diving block in the correct crouched position without it hurting, and I remember leaning on a bin to watch some of my friends' races because standing upright also caused pain. Needless to say, I didn't win that day or come close to a personal best. But I did learn two things:

1. an average teenage period slows a swimmer down approximately 0.56 seconds; and
2. non-applicator tampons should be discontinued.

When I was a young swimmer, I would ask myself, 'WWMSD' – 'What Would Michelle Smith Do?' – when I was struggling to get out of bed for an early-morning training session. I was absolutely heartbroken at the age of eight when the doping scandal broke during the 1996 Atlanta Olympics, and I got my answer. WWMSD? Tamper with a urine sample, apparently.

Michelle had been a hero for me and all of my swim team. She was someone we aspired to be like but not in an unachievable way. She wasn't a cartoon, she wasn't a millionaire, she didn't have magic powers or an unmentioned, unidentifiable source of income. She was real, she was Irish and she was possible.

More than anything else, *she* was a she. And then it all came crashing down. I sat in the pool with my friends surrounded by chlorine and cognitive dissonance as we tried to convince each other that it wasn't true. She wouldn't do something like that, they were just trying to sabotage her because people hate people who are successful. As it became less easy to convince ourselves of her innocence, we just stopped talking about her. We pinned our hopes and aspirations on female swimmers from the US and Australia. They didn't feel the same, though. They always felt like something from the telly. Maybe it was the accents.

I asked the Boy Housemate who his mentors are. Initially, and as expected, he said he had none, and off he went out the door with a stick over his shoulder, a red-and-white polka-dot pouch containing all his belongings tied to the end of it. When he returned he told me that he usually asks himself, 'What would my mother do?', in a given situation but then he usually *doesn't* do that thing. He says the best advice he gets is from what he imagines Judy Garland would tell him. He often asks himself, 'WWJGD'. He says the answer is almost always sweet and cutting. The Boy Housemate moves through his life leaving a detritus of confused and bruised victims in his wake.

As a young child, I followed the path of most kids and chose my mother and grandmother as my heroes/mentors. I think kids do this because the person who keeps you alive by keeping you in food and clean clothes is the greatest moral authority and also the most useful person to have onside.

Another mentor who had a profound influence on my early years came in cartoon form.

Disney's *The Lion King* is a treatise on mentorship. In the film, Mufasa is the father to young Simba and is a textbook mentor. Every other guru/sage/tutor/master/leader pales in comparison to Mufasa and the lengths he went to to provide his son with the guidance and support he needed to become the Lion King. He was so brilliant because he taught Simba lessons as well as rules. He taught him actual practical things that he needed to do, like how to pounce and how to catch prey. He taught him boundaries, literal and figurative: 'Everywhere the light touches, Simba, is our kingdom, but that shadowy place is beyond our borders, you must never go there.' I can't help but think that if Simba had just obeyed that rule, Mufasa might not have met his sticky end. But then there'd be no film.

He was also very philosophical, as good mentors often are: 'Being brave doesn't mean you have to go looking for trouble.'

The pinnacle of Mufasa's outstanding mentorship has to be the gesture of appearing to Simba in the clouds. If a mentor is willing to come back from the dead to appear to you when you need guidance, then they are the best mentor and should win all prizes.

I began to question my parental influence early and switched my allegiance to my first teacher. She knew the rules and all of the boundaries and, if you did what she said, then all was right with the world and you got an iced bun.

While Sabrina was my TV mentor, my fifth-class teacher was my first real-life mentor after my mother and grandmother.

Incidentally, it was Sabrina who made me fire her and go in search of someone new. I learned from Sabrina that the formula to find the slope of a line is: Y2 minus Y1 over X2 minus X1. When my fifth-class teacher couldn't show me how to use this formula (because it wasn't due to be on the curriculum for me for three more years), I got a pain in my stomach. This teacher, who had been my hero, came crashing down from her pedestal, art-deco pillars shrouding my hope for the future in a dust cloud.

I was on the hunt, yet again, for a role model. Various people, usually women, have since filled the role. All briefly, and some unbeknownst to themselves. Celine Dion's album *Falling Into You* was also my role model for a few years – a few powerful, high-octane, high-octave years.

I don't know when I developed a type of mentor. It's probably couched in something deep-rooted and psychological. The mentors who have guided me have had lots in common. If there were a Tinder-like app for mentors, I would swipe right on people who meet the following criteria.

1. They are old (or at least older than me).

That word 'old' is completely subjective. At thirteen, my 'old' mentors were thirty. Now I have mentors who are ninety and I feel like apologising to the woman who I classed as a geriatric when she was thirty.

The age rule lends itself to the second criterion.

2. They have to have vast amounts of life experience, usually in a specific field.

I have learned through trial and error that having a different mentor for different things is much safer. It's also less of a demand on the mentor to be unreasonably rounded in their experiences. I learned this the hard way when I asked my theatre mentor to help me with a tax return in 2011. It was an unreasonable ask that was destined to cause friction between me and him, and between me and Revenue.

3. They have to be smart, outstanding in their field.

Age and experience do not always equal intelligence or brilliance. In school, I never copied the homework of people who were less clever than me. Why would I do that? It's the same with mentors. I try to always be the least successful, intelligent or experienced person in a group. That way I'm always learning and aiming higher.

A desirable, though not essential, criterion is that a mentor be able to transfer their knowledge and experience, so they can be applied to situations that are unrelated to their area of expertise. This is a real bonus.

I started acting when I was sixteen. Up until then, I thought drama classes were for people who were bad at sport or who had a speech impediment. I wasn't wrong about the sports. When I got my first starring role in our transition-year opera *The Mikado*, and experienced the teamwork involved in putting on a show, I was hooked. The community and togetherness all the years of playing Super Nintendo one-player games and solo swimming couldn't give me, were delivered by the experience of theatre.

I guess I was lucky that I happened to be quite good at something I loved so much. I joined a youth theatre in Cork after transition year and thrived in the atmosphere created by Geraldine, the director. She was hands-off enough to make us feel like we were free to discover who we were, but very professional and demanding of our commitment to her shows. 'Commit or Quit' was a speech Geraldine used to give to people who were showing up late for rehearsals. I loved her and her rules so much.

I found people who worked professionally in the theatre industry attractive because they seemed to be running on passion. They certainly weren't doing it for the money. We live in a society that grossly undervalues the arts and so the people who are involved and successful are necessarily driven, ambitious and passionate about what they do. Geraldine taught me that when people are primed to dismiss you for being a non-essential part of society, you must never give them supportive evidence. People expect artists to be late, to be scatty, to be over-emotional and unbusinesslike. 'You must show up early, and be more professional and competent than your non-artist counterparts because that is the only way you will serve the arts and the generations of artists that have gone before you.'

I was fortunate to meet brilliant practitioners early in my acting career, before it even *was* a career. When I was eighteen, I worked with another director who refused to lower his demands on his actors because they were young. He said that youth was not an excuse for amateurism, and explained that he would be running our rehearsals and the subsequent production exactly as he would in the Abbey Theatre. His argument was that *he* was a professional and to expect anything less than the best from us was a slight on *his* reputation if nothing else.

In the show, I was playing an estate agent. I had lots of monologues and was on stage alone a lot of the time. This meant that during rehearsals I usually had an audience of fellow cast members watching my scenes being directed. I played each scene trying to make them laugh. In the beginning, they did, every time. I got so used to their laughter that I started to put a pause after the gag so I could relish it. After the sixteenth, seventeenth, eighteenth time they heard the jokes, they no longer found them funny. I tried to make myself louder, thinking maybe they just weren't *hearing* the joke. I tried to pause *before* it to make it land better. Seeing that I was getting frustrated, the director took me aside and said, 'Stefanie, stop trying to control their reaction and just focus on controlling your delivery. Don't make them laugh, make them hear.' That line has stuck with me since that day in the freezing cold church we rehearsed in. As a protégé-in-the-making, I was surprised, confused and finally silently impressed when, during the performance, I heard laughter from the wings. The cast found it funny again because I delivered the line as though I were saying it for the very first time.

After the hard lesson taught jointly by Sabrina and my fifth-class teacher, I have since tried to keep in mind that my mentors are human and struggle in their own lives. They're just trying to be 'adult' like me. But recently, I've noticed that something is happening – I've seen the twinkle of hope creeping into the corneas of the young people I interact with in the youth theatre in Mallow. The kids look to me as though I hold all of the answers and rules to how the world works just like I look to the people ahead of me for the same thing. I tell the kids not to make me a role model. I tell them I have no idea what I'm doing. I tell them I make massive mistakes all the time and I sometimes sit around waiting for people to text me back, just like they do. I find it terrifying that these little humans look to me as an example of how they should live their lives. It's a pressure that makes me cover my mouth when I curse in front of them. It's the pressure that made me hide behind trees when I used to smoke, even though I was legally allowed to, just because I didn't want to shatter their illusion of me. Spare me from the look of disappointment in a child's eyes when they realise you smoke. And yet I still turn to the adults around me to provide mentorship and guidance. Will I never learn?

Maybe it's safer to go back to *Sabrina the Teenage Witch* when I feel like my life needs to be reset. The TV show is unchanging. The dialogue isn't suddenly going to have a bad day and come crashing off its pedestal. It is what it is, and it will be thus forever, and I can't put that expectation of continuity and consistency on any one human. No one has all the answers and it's unfair of me to expect other people to set out the rules to regulate my life.

Hey … I think that's the most grown-up idea I've ever had.

Some time during that year in school, the rest of my friends became less interested in what 'teacher' had to say and switched their hero-allegiance to their peers. I didn't. I stayed in the role of teacher's pet for the rest of my schooldays. And it's a role I am still very comfortable playing.

Other kids grew up popping zits in front of posters of Justin Timberlake or David Beckham. I hung class pictures on my wall and re-read my school reports to see if the teachers liked me. As we reached our teenage years, my friends started to make decisions solely based on what would annoy the adults in their lives. I clung even more tightly to what was approved of, what was 'good', but I no longer cared so much about teachers. I moved on to coaches and theatre directors.

I sometimes adopt the habits of the people who are my mentors. One mentor I have at the moment is an extremely formidable, high-achieving, ambitious, powerhouse of a woman. I found out that one of the things that is tantamount to her success is getting up early, not concerning herself with what she is wearing, not eating breakfast and running on good coffee. I tried to take on all of those habits to try to operate at the level of productivity she does. I take what works for me and I leave the rest. I get up early, I choose my clothes the night before so I don't waste time in the morning with inconsequential decisions and I run on good coffee.

Unlike her, however, I need to eat breakfast or I get tired and cranky.

I have tested her ways, recognised what works for me and

adopted some as my own habits. Habits become lifestyles over time and that's when you start to see results in the areas that your mentors did.

My current mentor is brilliant, partially because I don't think she knows quite how much I rely on her. She knows that she has been cast in that role of 'advisor' though, and this helps massively. Great people know how to coach and mentor. It's almost like her personal success is not enough for her so she now tries to influence other people, to ignite them and motivate them towards unlocking their potential. She probably won't come back from the dead to appear to me in a cloud and guide me through my adulthood but she is definitely leaving her mark, as great mentors do. She has a vision of future-me and expects me to move towards it all the time.

I have one mentor whom I call the Voice of Reason. She probably wouldn't consider herself my mentor, because she is younger than me, and a close friend. I call on her when I have any intense emotion. If I am overjoyed, raging, devastated or too excited, I call the Voice of Reason to make sure I don't do anything in the heat of the moment. She has spared me many a drama.

As I age, I have a new appreciation for the family heroes I had when I was a kid. I see how hard my mother and grandmother worked and just how much was sacrificed to help me have the experiences that have led me to here.

I didn't learn until too late that my heroes were often complex people with flaws and issues and unflattering attributes. I was really hard on my mentors, knocking them off their pedestals for teeny-tiny mistakes. Mistakes as small as gravy granules or as inconsequential as wearing black and navy together. Rather than reconciling the moral discrepancies and accepting that heroes are human too, I wrote people off. This inevitably made me harder on myself because I was so hard on others for not being perfect. This is a defect I still have and have to be careful of. I am my own biggest critic and can be highly critical of other people when they don't appear to be the best of themselves.

I see politicians and captains of industry making mistakes and being lambasted for it. I see people crumbling in the face of not having all the answers, and I fear for the future. I think we have to create a context where it is OK and acceptable for a leader to put up their hands and say, 'I do not have all of the answers and I don't know the solution to this problem. Please can someone help me to find it?'. But because we don't allow people to say this, we force them to lie and pretend they know everything, which then leads them to being caught in that lie. Then we fire them and get the next person to hop onto the merry-go-round of delusion. It won't end well until we acknowledge that people – all people, no matter what age – struggle with life, wandering around the Monopoly board wondering how long is left until we all give up and accept that Monopoly is a stupid game that no one fully understands.

So while the mentor changes, the notion of having a mentor is a constant in my life I am very slow to let go of. It seems in any aspect of my life, when I need some guidance, someone appears to teach me whether they know it or not. I am fairly sure Nicole Scherzinger has no idea she is responsible for some of my most fashionable decisions to date.

Sometimes, I don't have all the knowledge I need, but I do have the knowledge that someone out there does, and that will never change. There is always someone out there to learn from.

7

DO YOU NEED A
PASSPORT TO LEAVE CORK?

IN 2009, AFTER I'D FINISHED COLLEGE, THE
recession in Ireland hit hard and the notion of moving away
from home became something very different for many people.
Lots of my friends who would have considered themselves
homebirds, who had absolutely no desire to move away, were
forced to board planes and leave, just to make a living.

There was a period of about a year after I finished in UCC
and moved to Dublin, where I was coming back to Mallow at

weekends to meet my closest friends. At going-away parties. The only time we would all be together was to say goodbye to one of us. I hated saying goodbye to people because of my childhood reaction and fear of change. I had moved to Dublin because there were simply no opportunities for me to get professional or vocational actor training in Cork. I didn't see it as 'leaving'. I saw it as moving up the road and I made a great effort to return and to keep in touch with my friends. I didn't understand why moving to Dublin wasn't enough for them. Why could they not just change province rather than hemisphere? When I heard of rooms to rent in Dublin, I would send links to my friends down in Cork to try to entice them to move up. I would have physically driven their stuff up and helped them with the move if I thought it would have kept them close and kept my circle of friends unbroken. I felt personally abandoned by the people who left.

I had been seeing a guy in UCC. I met him because he lived with a friend of mine. It was a very casual, almost tacit agreement that we were in a relationship. We never had the 'am I your girlfriend?' talk and a jury would have struggled to unanimously agree beyond reasonable doubt that we were ever official when we were in college, but we retrospectively agree that was our status back then. It doesn't really matter anyway, because when we decided that we actually were official, he decided quite quickly to break up with me to emigrate to Australia. Losing him on top of all the friends I had lost made me feel as though I wasn't enough to keep someone in a place.

I am very aware of how narcissistic that is, but show me a twenty-one-year-old who isn't self-absorbed. I struggled against the fact that the government or the economic circumstances were against me and my wish to keep everyone close to me at all times. It's hard to grow up in a time that is so far removed from your expectations. I think my generation are scared and reluctant to grow up from being Celtic Tiger cubs until the economic situation is returned to what we were told it was going to be.

At the time, the only way I could process what was happening was through my theatre work – which was in rhyme.

If people would stop leaving and moving away,
it would be easier for the ones who have to stay.
If we were all still here, we could carry the weight,
but a few people can't support an entire state.
And when you leave, you leave us behind
and we're alone, and lonely while we're trying to find
answers to problems that no one can fix,
that we didn't cause, and thrown into the mix
is a generation of young people going out of their heads,
feeling useless and burdened and a nuisance, instead
of being the youth of a glorious land,
who are nurtured and valued who can happily stand
on any world stage on their own two feet
and say, 'I believe in Ireland. Ireland is great!'
But instead they secretly buy tickets online,
to get out of the place, hundreds at a time.
They move to the sun, to get away from the cold,
away from the place where they thought they'd grow old.

In 2008, when I moved to Dublin to go to acting school, the city was far from normal for me. I had been in UCC for three years and was just getting comfortable living in Cork city. I had even started staying there from Monday to Friday (but never weekends). I had not yet spent a full week away from my mother's house and now I was going to move to DUBLIN. Anxiety was bubbling. My nana had always lived in Dublin, so I wasn't a stranger to the journey up, but my experience of Dublin with Nana was always in a car, predominately focused in Castleknock and Blanchardstown Shopping Centre. I had no experience of Dublin as a city, only as the backdrop to holidays and special occasions spent at Nana's house with the odd quick trip to the butcher or the Arnott's sale.

The entire city was like an airport. It was sprawling, international and cosmopolitan. I had been looking at Dublin on Google Maps from the moment I decided to move up. I rented an apartment above an Italian restaurant in Temple Bar. It was stupidly expensive but it was close to my acting school and I felt comforted that I could divide my time between my school and my apartment, and not have the scary concept of a commute. The bus to Nana's house went from outside my apartment too. That sealed the deal.

I was intimidated by the winding streets and roads named after people I'd never heard of. But, like the little yellow Google man, I dragged myself down to street view and started exploring. I felt tiny and terrified, but I did it anyway.

I tried to get to know the city on foot the day I arrived. It was a Monday. I went for my first walk around as a Dublin resident the day before starting my course. The first thing that strikes you when you move from Cork to Dublin in October is that it is BALTIC. Cork is damp, for sure, but it's balmy most of the time. The wind that cuts down whatever the name of that street is that brings you to the river from Jervis Street: that wind is killing Dublin tourism. That wind wants everyone who isn't an Arctic explorer to leave our nation's capital.

As I walked along that street, I noticed women selling fruit out of vintage prams. The prams are definitely worth more than whatever they're getting for their grapes. The women had to scream the fact that they were trying to trade because every passer-by had headphones in and was looking at the ground – I suspect in an attempt to protect their noses from frostbite. None of the perambulating public cared about the grapes or the humdrum that Monday morning. You could tell everyone was trying to get Hallowe'en out of the way so they could start looking forward to Christmas.

I never really enjoyed people-watching. My imagination can't move past the fact that it's slightly invasive to construct a narrative for an innocent, unaware citizen … (said the writer). But on that Monday in 2008, I was struck by the number of people walking around with individual soundtracks pumping in their ears.

I walked down Henry Street, calmed by seeing H&M, Zara, Lifestyle Sports, Nando's. The familiar. I got to the Spire and gazed up at it wondering whether its simplicity was profound or simply the result of a lack of imagination. I didn't think about it for too long before two men approached me separately. One asked me for spare change and the other asked me if I wanted a

Hop On, Hop Off Bus tour ticket. I told him, in a slightly shirty and offended tone, that I was not a tourist, that I actually *lived* here, so he could offer his ticket to someone else. He rebuffed with the fact that he hadn't seen too many residents of Dublin standing at the foot of the Spire and gaping up at it since its erection in 2003 and that I looked like a tourist. He also told me that no resident of Dublin would walk around 'The Northside' with their bag wide open, wallet exposed, and I should be careful. He left and my heart rate surged.

I legged it to the closest taxi rank. Walking up O'Connell Street, I stopped at Jesus-in-a-Box. The taxis were on strike but I hadn't noticed their pickets because I was confronted with the Sacred Heart of Jesus staring at me from inside a Perspex box. A kind but extremely racist taxi driver explained the reason for the strike and then told me that, apparently, during the Civil War, the horse-drawn cab drivers had salvaged all the stuff from the shops on O'Connell Street and left them in the middle of the street for the owners to reclaim. But no one ever collected Jesus, so they put him in a box and he has remained there to this day. It was a nice story, tarnished slightly by his feelings towards 'foreigners stealing his fares'. He did direct me back to the safety of Temple Bar, though. On my way, I was offered a *Metro* newspaper and enjoyed my accurate horoscope reading over a Starbucks coffee.

We didn't have Starbucks in Cork at the time, or at least I had never seen one, and that was the first thing that made me feel like I had made the right choice. Real actors drank Starbucks from take-away cups. I had arrived.

If an acting course with similar industry attention and respect had been offered in Cork, I would never have moved. I auditioned for four of the most prestigious drama schools in London and was accepted by two of them. I was only kidding myself, teasing myself, thinking that I would ever have been able for a move to London, but it served the purpose of giving perspective and context. Having the option of London made the move to Dublin less intimidating. It's like when you're buying, a coat, say. There's one for €200, one for €400 and one for €600. You settle on the €400 one because it's better quality and a more valued investment than the €200 one, but you didn't lose the run of yourself completely and go for the flashy one. That's the only reason the €600 one is on sale in the first place – to provide a comforting comparison that secures your decision to buy the €400 coat.

I moved to Dublin because I saw more opportunities for myself up here. 'Yeah, buts' had crippled me from making the move three years previously.

Never had more damaging and debilitating words come to me.

'Yeah, but … what about debt?'

'Yeah, but … what if I feel lost in the city?'

'Yeah, but … what if I hate it?'

'Yeah, but … what if I can't get a job?'

Moving into my room in the apartment in Temple Bar and attending my acting course was almost like hitting pause on real life for another two years.

I was still very much in college-mode. I gathered my bedsheets when they needed washing and hopped on the 37 bus with a gear bag full of laundry, swanned into my nana's house and filled up on the contents of her fridge while my clothes were washed and tumble dried. It wasn't until 2010 when I moved out of Temple Bar and into a house with my two friends that I really learned what it's like to live away from home. In the other places, I had been simply renting a room, the concerns of the physical house were not mine – my name wasn't even on the lease in those places. As soon as the heating bill is in your name, you know shit's got real.

The Girl Housemate and I decided we would look for a house together. She is also from Mallow and was moving up to start a career in fashion journalism. She'd been a few years behind me in school but we had been friends through drama and music. We were the perfect balance of friends and strangers that is ideal for living together. We weren't lifelong friends, so didn't have that overfamiliarity that leads to annoying habits being overlooked and positive traits being exploited – we knew each other well enough to eat each other's food but not well enough to do it without replacing it.

We found our dream house on the northside of Dublin after seeing some abominations I wouldn't keep a pet rat in. There was one problem. It was a three-bed. The Girl Housemate piped up when the estate agent told us there was another viewing in two hours, 'No, no, we'll take it. I have a friend who I am sure will move in with us.'

She told me his name and that he was also from Mallow. I hadn't heard of him. She called his phone four times but he didn't answer. He was working in River Island in Cork at the time. I decided to go to the source. We called the River Island phone. He answered.

The Girl Housemate said, 'Hi. I'm viewing a house in Dublin. It's a three-bed. Do you want to move in with me and Stefanie Preissner?'

Apparently he knew me well enough to say, 'Sure.'

At that point, sight unseen, he became the Boy Housemate. He moved up with all of his stuff eight days later. Those eight days were just enough time for us to move in and put our female stamp on the place. We did the human equivalent of canine territorial marking – we metaphorically peed all over the house for over a week. It was also just enough time that the Boy Housemate would never feel like the house was as much his as it was ours. To this day he feels this way. It was in this little terraced house where I began to learn who I was – really a nightmare to live with.

I watch my housemates when they're filling the kettle and have to bite my lip when they fill it more than they need. If they happen to go to the toilet or leave the kitchen when it's boiling, I have been known to run over and pour some out. I like to think it's a virtuous gesture and helping to save the planet. Sometimes, I will pretend I need something so I can leave the room and turn off their bedroom lights because they leave them on. If it weren't a criminal offence, I would put a camera in the bathroom because one of them squeezes our communal toothpaste in such a way that leaves crusty toothpaste residue all over the top of it and the other one uses way too much toilet paper.

The tongue is bitten off me.

In the past eight years, since I moved to Dublin, I've thought about ways to deal with this. I have fantasies about leaving passive-aggressive notes on the dirty dishes saying things like, 'Oh if only there were a way to get this grease off me.' I once thought of writing *A Housemate Haiku* on a particularly stellar pile of dishes:

Week-old, caked-on flakes
Lining my paella dish
Oh – it's your porridge.

Or maybe it would be more powerful to prop all the empty toilet rolls together on top of the toilet seat so they'd *actually* have to move them to use the toilet. But I am far too sweet to ever do such a thing.

I hope they read this book, though. Get your shit together, guys.

I'm at my most controlling when it comes to the washing machine. I love putting on a wash. It calms me. Ever since I was a kid, watching the washing machine spinning around and around, the colours swirling and the rhythm created by the vibration, the white noise sound of it – fills me with an amniotic comfort and soothes me like nothing else can. This, coupled with my overly sensitive sense of smell, means that if a wash is put on with the wrong detergent and at a time when I don't get to watch it for even a few minutes I get a little miffed.

One of the hardest lessons I have learned since moving out of home is this: Room-mates turn your whites pink. Your mother never does that.

Apart from those few little things, living away from home is the best adult change in my life.

As Kevin McCallister once said in *Home Alone*, 'I made my family disappear.' *eyebrows dance*

Ah, the Irish Rail announcement at Mallow. Nothing says 'Welcome Home' or 'See you at Christmas' quite like it.

'Passengers for Banteer, Millstreet, Rathmore, Killarney, Farranfore and Tralee please change at Mallow. Mallow is the next stop.'

And there's nothing like a few nights at Mam's for the casual comforts of home.

I start to forget the most basic survival skills that I manage no problem when I am in Dublin. I leave the house without my coat, I forget my keys and my voice gets three degrees more whiney. I always seem to get sick when I go home. Maybe it's the dust in my uninhabited bedroom, but I get a cough and the sniffles. My mother is able to identify of which provenance the cough is. It's usually either chesty or tickly. I am rarely struck down with a dry cough. Thank God.

The fridge is packed with food that's packed with nutrients. Brand names scream at you from every shelf and you get to substitute Choco Rice with Coco Pops, and you swear you can taste the difference. Coco Pops are Bae. The heating is on a timer and the house is always warm, bills don't cross your mind because they're not your problem and so you prance around in one layer of clothing, enjoying the freedom of movement without the restriction of two coats, a scarf and a dressing gown.

At home, after a night out, there's always a hot-water bottle in my bed. It's those little touches that make me wonder why I ever left. But then I leave the immersion on or my coffee mug on the floor next to the couch 'for later' and I suddenly remember all the reasons I love being in Dublin. I try to log on to Netflix and am confronted with a remote control from the Middle Ages and the broadband doesn't work, so I go seeking out the closest thing to 3G I can find in Mallow and look up Irish Rail to see how quickly I can get back to civilisation. No amount of roast chickens or surprise hot-water bottles will replace Netflix, fibre broadband or, if you're really lucky, the relationships you develop with your housemates.

After all these years of living with my friends, we're like that old IKEA ad where they're all in the kitchen and throwing knives and mayonnaise over their shoulders and catching things without looking because they're *so* used to each other and their routine that they all fit together like a neat Scandinavian-designed Russian doll.

I sometimes wish it could be *actually* like those matryoshka dolls where the biggest one keeps all the littler ones safe inside it. When you're growing up, you are housed, cocooned, encased in your home and there's a protection in that. So on one hand, the freedom of living away from home is great, but it's also potentially dangerous.

I often wake up and leave the house before either of my

housemates are awake. I catch myself around lunch-time wondering if they are alive when I haven't heard from them. I've told them about this and it led to a discussion about how long we would have to not be in touch with one another before we called the guards and filed a missing person's report.

I live a structured and routinised life. I wake up every morning at 4:30 a.m. Before my eyes are open, I reach around my bed to find my phone. I check the news, my horoscope and any texts/WhatsApps or mails, and then I sit up in the bed. Around 4:45 a.m., I turn on my bedside lamp and light the scented candle next to my bed. I go to the bathroom and on the way I flick the switch on the kettle. I finish in the bathroom, make a coffee and bring it back into my room. I am upright, at my laptop, typing, by 5 a.m. I write until I hear one of my housemates or until 7:30 a.m. Then, I get up, turn on *Ireland AM* and make my porridge. I have another coffee with my breakfast and watch the TV. I then get dressed, leave the house and am writing in some local coffee shop by 9 a.m. On Tuesdays and Thursdays, I go to my kickboxing class in Martial Arts Inc. It's exceptionally rare that I stray from this pattern. I would be very easy to kidnap. And I've just made it easy for any potential stalkers.

During our chat about when we would ring the guards, my friends said that if they woke up and *Ireland AM* wasn't on the TV or my bowl and mug from breakfast weren't in the kitchen, they'd probably text me to check. If I didn't respond within an hour (I'm always on my phone), they'd take action.

The Girl Housemate is almost as predictable. Her mornings

have a strong routine that usually involves the smell of turkey bacon and the lingering scent of L'Oréal in the bathroom. She's often out late at night, but she always comes home to sleep. If she wasn't there in the morning and hadn't sent a text, I would certainly be worried.

The Boy Housemate is destined to die alone in the Wicklow Mountains. He often disappears for days at a time. He never responds to text messages and often leaves his phone off for days. The fact that he is rarely anywhere other than work or home or buying cigarettes in the Spar in between those two places makes it a little easier to track him down, but there are phases, usually around payday, where he can be unaccounted for for days and no one has any idea when or if he will be back.

I'm sure his controlled living environment, aka me, is part of the reason he disappears sporadically. I imagine him like a pressure cooker building up with the desire for freedom and then running screaming towards the sea trying to escape the confines I put on him. It's dangerous, though, because if our lives ever took a Scandinavian turn and he was taken, it would be days upon days before I rang the guards, if ever. He usually shows up unfazed just as I'm cooking dinner. That would probably be the first thing I would do if I thought he was gone. Try to lure him back with the smell of carbonara.

I felt like a little grape picked off the bunch and tossed into a massive fruit salad when I moved to Dublin. But by sticking it out and getting some support networks up here in the form of work and friends, I adapted. Slowly.

Dublin is my home because I made it work, not because I was born here. Dublin is my home because I am here. The move was traumatic and exciting and now I see how necessary it was.

It was important to learn how to compromise and negotiate.

It was important to discover the value of money and the price of electricity units.

It was important to realise that people are more than the sum of their annoying quirks.

It was important to realise other people need to go off the radar for a few days for their self-preservation.

It was important to learn if the washing machine goes through a cycle without me, I will still be OK.

And it's lovely when you learn you can live with other people's family members, in someone else's house, in a city you are not from and still feel like you utterly belong.

Eh, have I just accepted that *some* changes are OK? Or even that some changes might even be good? Oh, God. Is it too late to change the title of this book?

8

UPLOADED
DOWN UNDER

IN FEBRUARY 2014, I WAS ON TOUR IN AUSTRALIA. I had written a show called *Solpadeine Is My Boyfriend* for the 2012 Dublin Fringe Festival. The show was about how one girl copes when her boyfriend emigrates to Australia and her primary relationship becomes one with the over-the-counter painkiller, Solpadeine. The show got a great reception at Dublin Fringe and subsequently toured all over Ireland – it was also translated into Romanian for its European premiere in Bucharest, but the real coup was being invited to the World Theatre Festival in Brisbane. So many Irish people living in Australia at the time meant an increased demand for Irish arts out there. The irony of benefiting from the loss of my friends and boyfriend was not lost on me. It's the pinnacle of most performance artists' careers to tour their work on other continents, and I was honoured to have been asked. If you looked at it from the outside, I had a hit one-woman show, I was in a different hemisphere, I was getting great to good reviews, I was in high demand and tanning beautifully. It was every theatre-maker's dream.

Or at least it seemed that way, going on how I was reporting it on social media.

For a time, on this trip, the reality and the online version were the same. I was uploading as I went. People from home were texting me: 'OMG it looks so fab, you're having a ball', 'So jealous of your tan. Congrats on the reviews.'

But then something happened. I had a panic attack in the dressing room after a lunch-time performance. You know when you run or jog and then you stop and your chest is kind of burning, as if you've had a shot of straight whiskey, and you can't catch your breath? It was like that, but I hadn't been running.

It came out of nowhere. Sitting in front of the mirror, my knuckles turned white around the seat of my chair. I'm not sure exactly why it happened and it hasn't happened since but, at the time, it was crippling. My chest felt like it was corrugated iron, all crumpled up in spasm, and I couldn't get air into my lungs. I don't think I was any more stressed than I usually was, I hadn't had any major problem or grief or trauma in the days or hours leading up to the event. I was missing home a little, concerned about the reviews and the reception of the show, I guess. One review had called me 'a very large girl' and maybe I was more affected by that than my water-off-a-duck's-back response had let on. But to this day, I do not blame any one thing for the panic attack. I'm still baffled about how it happened and often wonder if I'll be somewhere one day and be caught off-guard again.

I was given the name of the doctor in the medical centre near the festival hub and was seen to within the hour. The kind doctor spoke to me about panic attacks and how various hormones swim around your body and how, sometimes, the levels get messed up and turn you into the kind of shaky, quivering mess I had presented to him. He said I needed to take it easy, be gentle with myself and get my supports around me to help me relax.

I spoke to my producers, and decided the best option was to go home. We thought it better to err on the side of caution because the doctor had said I had been lucky the panic attack hadn't triggered an asthma attack and that I should really try to reduce my stress. On this recommendation, fearing a surprise asthma attack, we called it quits. I felt really awkward and embarrassed about it. I had trained for years to be an actor and now, on what was only my third professional show, at twenty-five, it looked like I wasn't able for it. I felt pathetic.

Remember that game show *The Crystal Maze* where you get locked into the game when you fail and all your friends watch you for a minute and then leave you there on your own? That's what I felt was going to happen. I had travelled with a stage manager who was supportive of my decision to go home. He planned to travel from Brisbane down the coast to visit some friends and family anyway, so he didn't care. He offered to go with me to the airport but I declined. I had been there two weeks at that stage and had done all the performances of the show I was committed to doing at the World Theatre Festival. I was booked to speak at some events and to meet other presenters who were interested in buying my show for their festivals, but those meetings never happened.

I made a decision the following day at Brisbane airport not to tell anyone that I was coming home. I ran to an airport shop and took photos of some postcards and saved them on my phone. I would later upload them to Facebook to make it look like I was visiting all of these Australian landmarks. Looking back on it now, it seems a pretty resourceful and clever thing to do, but it betrays how insecure I was about my online image.

I look at myself today and know beyond all reasonable doubt there is no way I would think twice about what other people think of my decision to leave a place where I wasn't comfortable. That's a change I can definitely cope with.

When I arrived in Singapore after the first leg of my flight, I uploaded the first lie. I tagged myself at Ayers Rock and uploaded the photo of Uluru that was on the postcard. Straight away I got a response: 'That looks like magic. You're so lucky. #jealous.' I calmed immediately. It was working.

By the time I got to my house in Dublin, I had virtually visited the Great Barrier Reef, Sydney Harbour Bridge and some island that I can't guarantee isn't New Zealand.

Each uploaded photo fooling my 800 closest friends that I

was happy, joyous and free, navigating the Australian Outback like Bear Grylls, turning a gorgeous shade of leather and eating witchetty grubs for sustenance. The reality was that I was in bed, in Dublin, with no prospect of any visitors because for me to call for company and support would uncover the lie and ruin the illusion. Because my housemates happened to be on holidays at the time, I stayed like that for a week.

After a week, the jet lag had worn off and my original flight to Ireland was about to land. As the wheels touched down in Dublin airport, I pulled my duvet over my head and took two painkillers. How was I meant to deal with everyone asking me about all of the places I had visited, and all of the things I had seen?

I uploaded another postcard picture. This time it was of a hand holding a dripping ice-cream next to the entrance sign of the Steve Irwin Zoo. What if people asked? I hadn't been anywhere near that zoo. I had, however, watched the entire series of *Planet Earth* and eaten about fifty litres of ice-cream since coming home. I felt a massive pressure to project only my best – albeit unrealistic – self in a virtual version of keeping up with the Joneses.

I hadn't thought this through. In trying to keep up a false narrative of my life, I had inadvertently created something that I could never live up to in real life.

The comments were coming in, people 'dying to catch up and hear all about it'. I couldn't cope. I couldn't do it. Lying online was easy but I couldn't keep it up face to face. People would see right through me, they'd know I was a liar, they'd stop being my friends. I needed to escape from it all, to run away, to disappear. So I did the most drastic thing a millennial can do. I deleted my Facebook page.

In the beginning, Facebook was everything I love in one place. I joined in 2007 and, at nineteen, I quickly loved the way I could use it to keep tabs on people, compare myself to them, see who was going out with who, monitor where tensions were building and look at the various heart-shaped designs on cappuccino froth. But slowly, inexorably, Facebook started to suck the joy out of my life. It didn't have to suck too hard, mind you, because I just uploaded my joy directly onto the site and left nothing for myself. I was constantly comparing my whole life to the best bits of everyone else's, and it became draining.

The withdrawals from quitting Facebook were intense. The feeling of validation and aliveness you feel by constantly comparing yourself to other humans is a powerful thing. Without it, initially, you do start to question your own real-ness. 'If I don't upload this photo of me in the gym, was I even really at the gym?' It made me acutely aware of an unspoken motto of my generation: 'a calorie shared is a calorie halved'. The little joys in life are amplified by sharing them with your 800 nearest and dearest.

I remember the first time I changed my Facebook relationship status to 'In a Relationship'. I was twenty-two and had been seeing 'Stephen' on and off for three years. Off mostly.

At one point, one of the criteria for getting back together was that we could announce it on Facebook. He was reluctant and I took this as him being embarrassed by me. I now realise he was just a make-fewer-announcements kind of guy. Being able to publicly announce it was actually more important to me at that time than being in the relationship itself. I was more concerned about how my friends felt about the man I was with than whether or not I even liked him. I would have gone out with Kermit the Frog if it meant the gushing approval of my friends.

Then, the moment came when we broke up. The shame again. The excited comments and giddy emojis that the relationship had provoked online disappeared. People are far less quick to comment on a sad status. So, instead of reaching out after a break-up, instead of gathering my friends around me by telling them the trauma I was feeling, I quietly hid my relationship status from my profile so that no one would notice. Or if they did, they could easily pretend they hadn't and wouldn't be forced to soothe me.

When I deleted my page completely, I constantly felt like everyone I knew was hanging out without me. The isolation and FOMO (fear of missing out) were all-consuming. I felt like I was missing out on life – and not just other people's lives but my own life too, because so much of my life had become about the instant gratification of 'likes'. I used to upload a funny status, having slaved over it for minutes and, when it got the attention I was aiming for, it was like millennial heroin. Completely addictive.

Maybe the panic attack in Australia was because the reviews weren't as good as I was pretending they were or as good as I had expected them to be. All the Irish reviews had been glowing.

The curated social media stuff was painting this perfect picture of this award-winning show and it was threatened by one online review that anyone who had a Facebook page – i.e. internet access – could see. Maybe I'm drawing connections where there are none. But maybe that review was the first wobbling domino that collapsed the whole illusion. If your entire identity is tied in to what you do for a living, and someone criticises it or it's somehow threatened, the consequences are understandably profound.

Being labelled an 'attention seeker' on Facebook is akin to being labelled a witch in Salem back in the day. I noticed when I was on Facebook that a funny, relatable post like 'When you're dying to pee but it's too cold to get out of bed' would get significantly more positive attention than a post where I was being honest and open and real. In general, people who upload things like 'I'm having the worst day ever and I'm really struggling' get a response from a friend they haven't seen since third class saying, 'You OK, hun?.' This helps very little. When someone reaches out on Facebook they don't want just *anyone* to respond. The people they *do* want to target have likely taken a screenshot of the pathetic post and sent it to a WhatsApp group along with an eye-roll emoji.

But what if you *are* looking for attention? When did that become such a bad thing? Sometimes we need attention, sometimes loneliness and being overwhelmed can be terminal if not given the right attention.

If your Facebook profile is a digital extension of your life, then it's dangerous to upload only the best parts. It's the equivalent of those poor babies in the Romanian orphanages who don't cry anymore because they know that even if they do, no one will come. They end up emotionally stunted and with massive mental health problems.

Social media can put a distorted lens on how we project ourselves to the world. For obvious reasons, people do not advertise their negative traits on their social profiles or post pictures that are unflattering. How many times have you asked or been asked not to put a photo on Facebook?

Because of this strict control of the way we are viewed, we are often fooled into believing other people's lives are much better than our own; that people are prettier or more successful than us. What is essential to remember is that they, too, wear masks – the way I do, the way everyone does.

For me, the cons outweighed the pros. But, sometimes, I try to figure out if maybe I am missing out on stuff by abstaining from Facebook. My friendships definitely need that extra bit of effort because no communication is by chance. It puts a lot of pressure on 'catch-ups' over coffee when I have to update someone on everything that has happened since I last saw them and vice versa. If I were on Facebook, I'd already know their basic news so I'd be able to decide where I wanted more info and which stories I'd rather avoid.

I miss one aspect – the ability to structure a conversation with a friend based on things you know about them from Facebook so you can avoid putting your foot in it.

'How's John getting on?'

'He's dead, Stefanie.'

Awkward encounters are inevitable when you erase Mark Zuckerberg from your life, but I just can't bring myself to go back. So often now I experience JOMO, the joy of missing out – I see things on Instagram or Twitter and I get this ecstatic wave of relief that I am not attending the damp, muddy festival du jour.

I also feel #privileged not to have Facebook dredging up the past at me every day. It goes back through your page like an archaeological dig to tell you what you were doing this time five years ago. So you realise you were happier/skinnier/less single/ more tanned/more free than you are now – or, even worse, you might realise you are exactly the same.

In the days leading up to deleting my Facebook account, I paid particular attention to the types of comments that were popping up on my timeline. There is no one particular person or one particular comment that sent me over the edge – it was just the pattern of unhappiness and discontent that was being delivered to me every moment that I felt I could do without.

A typical scroll through my newsfeed revealed people I barely knew anymore, protesting to like-minded people about things that offended them.

Hungry for a fight with people they call friends
about things they probably could fix,
but lack the effort.
'Stop stoning women in eastern Iran.'
'Child goes missing after man sees White Van.'
'Forty-year-old man missing in County Cork.'

'New credit card fraud pattern hits New York.'

'Save a child with cancer with 4,000 likes.'

'F**K THE DOPES WHO STOLE MY BIKE.'

'Does anyone have an apartment to let?'

'I can't cope with the rain, my UGG boots are wet.'

'Please vote for this photo taken by a pal of mine.'

'WE NEED TO DO SOMETHING ABOUT PALESTINE.'

'When you throw chewing gum, a bird thinks it's bread!'

'Bombing in Syria, 10,000 dead.'

'Don't stop and give directions to a forlorn stranger.'

'PLEASE SHARE this or your children are in danger.'

'Good morning, Facebook, what's the panic du jour?'

'Cancer makes money, they're hiding the cure.'

'CLICK LIKE if you support gay rights.'

'Does anyone know where I can find cheap flights?'

'Fight obesity, give kids child-size portions.'

'I HAVE AN OPINION ABOUT ABORTION.'

My newsfeed filling with angry words from angry heads

written with angry fingers in angry beds.

Sitting on couches, couched in inertia

sit back and complain that they've all deserted you.

Everyone says 'NO' in Helvetica Bold,

no to Leo, no to Donald, to tax on the household.

To pay cuts and pay increases and property tax,

writing 'NO' on Facebook isn't changing the facts.

They can't do simple maths like long division,

but they have the solution to direct provision.

'Bondholders are scum and why won't the ministers listen

to my Facebook post, I'm writing on my own in my kitchen?'
'Socialism is brilliant – let's all hold hands.'
'Quick there's an ethical issue in Africa – I'M WITH THE
    BAND.'
Don't say no one's listening to you when they can't even hear
because you're not opening your mouth, your laptop has no
    ears.
'Occupy Sesame Street, Big Bird's Obese.'
'Why is my dole getting f**king decreased?'
'Minister X is a criminal because he gave a raise to his
    daughter!'
'LET'S SET FIRE TO THE B*ST**DS AT IRISH WATER!'
'Keep calm sure it's grand, we've a German ATM.'
Spewing money, we forget we have to pay back to them.
Money doesn't grow on trees and yet banks have branches,
but they break when you climb trees, there are no more chances.

In 1984, George Orwell predicted the major fear in the future
would be that Big Brother was watching. It strikes me now that,
during my lonely week in Australian–Irish limbo, my biggest
fear was that no one was watching me at all.

By creating a false self online, I nearly uploaded myself out
of reality. I'm still under the influence of Twitter and Instagram,
and I've recently got attached to Snapchat, but I'll cross the
Sydney Harbour Bridge only when I come to it.

9

SITUATIONSHIPS

WHILE I WAS WRITING THIS CHAPTER, I ASKED THE Boy Housemate if he believed in love. Without looking at me, he let go of the spoon he was holding and it dropped back into the near-empty tub of Ben and Jerry's. He doesn't have a favourite flavour and he is not brand loyal. His tastes are 100 per cent dictated by the whims of the supermarket's Deal of the Week.

'Is that a trick question, Stefanie?'

'No.'

'I do not believe in love. Love is not real. I believe in Marxian exchange relationships.'

'What?'

'It's what you and I have. All love is vampiric capital.'

'Did you just tell me you love me?'

The Boy Housemate got up and went to his room, pretending to vomit. He sent me a WhatsApp from the other side of the wall, not three feet away from me:

I'll never love myself and 'If you can't love yourself, how in the hell you gonna love somebody else?' – RuPaul.

Then he had a sugar crash and fell asleep.

I don't know if I've ever been in love. I think I have been. The only way I can tell is because I had a physical feeling in my chest when I would see his name pop up on my phone. It wasn't butterflies, though, and that's what all my friends and all contemporary cinema said I should feel. It felt a bit like indigestion. You're not really sure how it happened, you can't quite describe it, you're not sure how long it will last, but it's very good at making itself felt. Waking up and knowing you love someone and you are loved by them is like having one of those hand warmers in your pocket all day.

But eventually hand warmers go cold.

Love is the best ever. Until you lose it. Or it loses you.

Why do other people get to make decisions that impact my life? This sort of change is particularly frustrating. It's especially potent when it's a break-up. One person wants to be in the relationship and one person doesn't. Why does one of those desires get to override the other? Why do we have to break up just because *you* want to? It's so unfair. We saw it on a global level recently when Northern Ireland and Scotland voted against Brexit but are being dragged out of Europe because it's what English people want.

But we can't change other people or make them do what we want them to. That's the super power I would choose, given the option. Mind control.

Does that make me a psycho?

There's nothing quite like being broken up with to make you feel like the loneliest person on earth. You start to resort to all sorts of things to alleviate the loneliness – I find that watching a horror film always makes me feel like I'm not alone in the house.

But how quickly we forget. It's like childbirth. When you have overcome heartache, it's hard to empathise with other people who are going through it in that moment. I think it's a form of self-preservation. But, for the record, and that we may help fellow sufferers, this is how I remember it.

I've written it in the second person because I think it's a collective experience.

The alarm rings. You were having a dream about your teeth falling out, you gasp for air and hold your mouth when you wake. Brief relief as you realise it's not real, and then it hits you. The reality is worse. For a split second, you had forgotten what happened yesterday. Your stomach fills with a heavy … something … and the place where you learned your heart is when you were in school, is sore, genuinely a physical pain. Every way you try to describe it has already been said. You're heartbroken. No, it's aching. Heartache. *This* is heartache.

You sit up in the bed and make a decision not to be a cliché.

Not to be a stereotype. You have been broken up with. That is all. People break up all the time and no one dies in pairs, so at some stage everyone loses someone, whether they leave or die. They're gone. You can totally cope with this. It's completely, totally normal.

But it doesn't feel normal.

It feels like no one in the world has ever felt this discomfort. You can't actually believe the audacity of time. The idea that time is demanding to go on, the notion that this day is going to happen with or without you. You remember some remnant of a Leaving Cert poem about 'bells tolling for thee' and some man … or woman … who wanted the clocks to stop. You reckon, if you could remember the poem at all, you'd really relate right now. Fucking Leaving Cert.

The pain in your chest is so real that you spend a few minutes while brushing your teeth trying to describe it without using clichés. You go on WebMD and it tells you to go to a hospital. You put down your phone. No texts from him anyway.

The pain is round and solid and sits in a ball in your chest just to the left of where the joy sat.

Don't be a cliché. Don't be a stereotype.

You consider the shower. The water would act as a veil for the tears that seem to come so freely. But then the thought of the million little droplet assassins hitting your naked flesh on what is a morning too filled with adverse conditions. No. No, you'll skip the shower. A spritz of Batiste dry shampoo and two extra spritzes of perfume will do it.

A yoghurt for breakfast. The women in yoghurt ads have

never been broken up with. They're too pure and serene and undamaged to have ever experienced this sort of pain. I wonder will anyone ever look at me the way Nicole Scherzinger looks at a Müller Corner.

On your walk to the bus, you snap your headphones out of your ears during the first two bars of 'Someone Like You'. Sorry, Adele, you don't get to sing to me today. You know too much. You're like that terrible kindness offered by an older woman, when they tilt their head and ask, 'Are you all right?', and then you burst into tears because for some reason this pain gets worse when people are kind.

Maybe if everyone was horrible to you today, it would be more palatable. Maybe the rejection by society at large would reflect the rejection you feel inside and the parallel would be comforting. Somehow, the kindness of strangers and friends seems so incongruous that it is contemptuous. You just want them to leave you alone to be fucking sad.

You climb onto the bus. The bus driver greets you with a smile and a 'Howya, love?' You feel the tears clogging up the back of your throat and you nod, walking on, wondering what it is about men who work in the service industry and their ability to make you share your darkest secrets with them. 'Darkest secrets' – don't be a stereotype, don't be a cliché.

You sit on the bus and look out the window. It's the same seat you sit in whenever it's free but, today, it's different. There's an armrest you usually lean on so you can text. Your hand falls naturally into this position and you feel like you might vomit or cry or both as you realise you can't text him. You don't have anyone to text. Well, you do, but you're just not ready to start the post-mortems and responding to the deluge of regurgitated support from friends. It's like one girl once got advice from someone about a break-up and, since that day, it has been passed around like a terrible chain letter. The Chinese Whisper Syndrome replacing the pertinent details so you feel it's been crafted for you.

'I know it doesn't feel like it now, but this will pass, it will get easier. Hang in there. I'm here for you. Call me if you need anything.'

Your phone in your hand feels impotent and useless, you forget momentarily that it has uses other than texting, calling and holding photos of him.

Netflix. You use his account. You wonder if he's changed his password, thereby signing you out. You rush to the black and red app to check. What fucking folder is it in? There it is in the Utilities folder with your period-tracking app. You try not to cry thinking about how you won't need that for a while either. Right now, it feels like you'll never need it again. That somehow this break-up is the equivalent of menopause for ending your future hopes. You tap the app. It opens and his name pops up under the photo of him. Of course he hasn't signed you out because he is good and kind and he still hasn't done anything wrong. If he could just do something wrong then you could tell people he is a prick and a bastard and then you could all sit around burning pictures of him and sticking needles in voodoo dolls made in his likeness. It strikes you that a voodoo doll in his likeness would be easier to come by than a hard copy of a photograph to burn.

You get off the bus, you bury your hands deep in your pockets. Fingers still gripped around your phone just in case he rings and you need to answer within a second. On the street, it seems that everyone has the same ringtone as you. Over and over, you glance at your screen, you are certain you heard your message alert. But, no. You curse Steve Jobs for the ubiquity of Tritone and Marimba and hate yourself a little for being such a generic consumer.

Walking down Grafton Street. There's a busker playing 'Wonderwall'. You've never heard that overplayed song in a meaningful way before and it certainly wasn't one of 'your songs' with him but, because you're so sad, the idea of any song at all catches in the back of your throat like a gulp of salt water. Don't be a cliché. Don't be a stereotype.

Then you pass the actual memories, and they feel different.

The things that society tells you are meant to make you feel sad – the songs you listened to, the other couples holding hands, the mother pushing her child on a swing that reminds you that you will never have a family unit with that man – are all fake feelings. They feel nothing like the withering hollow that the real memories induce. When you are queuing to pay for a salad and you turn around and catch the smell of him and you cannot go on because, for a moment, you think he's right there, and what would you even say? When you see the restaurant you had breakfast in the first morning and you get the urge to go in and ask them to take the eggs Benedict you shared off the menu because for anyone else to order it from now on would tarnish it forever and you feel compelled to demand that the world stops for just one second to acknowledge your loss.

But you can't.

You get to your desk and the banality of your job sends your imagination into overdrive. What if he showed up at the office to get you back? What if you got hit by a car and gave his number at the hospital? Then he would have to come. You imagine all of the situations that would make him break his commitment to 'having some space to get used to being apart'.

When your store of hope has been run dry by your imagination, you start going over the facts. The facts of yesterday. You replay the fight and the break-up over and over in your head.

That part is possibly the worst and the most draining. Maybe it's because I am a writer, so my imagination is primed to be more ... active ... dramatic ... self-deprecating and crippling ... but during that 'replay' phase, I turned my break-up and previous fights over in my head so many times that they practically rhymed.

I'm going to call my fake boyfriend in the following bit 'Stephen' (with a *ph*). My name is spelled with an *f* and I get really shirty when people spell it wrong. I feel like Stephanie with a *ph* is like the less successful and more generic version of me, so I'm going to channel all of my feelings towards the misspelling of my name into this character, Stephen.

I met Stephen at a house party and, when the first big fight came, it was close to Christmas. I have to admit, I thought he was trying to break up with me to get out of having to buy me a present. But, no.

After ten months we had our first fight,
we hadn't quite worked out how to argue right.
Stephen was upset and couldn't get work,
had a degree that was just paper, he was going berserk.
And all of his friend were posting photos online,
of lying in the sun and being drunk all the time.
He was getting so angry, so deeply unhappy,
shouting at me, being nasty and snapping.
—*'Ya, well, if you weren't keeping me here, I'd be gone!'*
—*'So leave, Stephen. Do what you want!'*
—*'I can't do what I want because there's no fucking jobs.'*
—*'You haven't applied in months 'cause you're a snob*
and you're being too picky about the work that you'll take!'
—*'I am a trained engineer, for Jesus' sake!*
I'm entitled to work in the field that I trained.'
—*'You're not entitled to anything. Do you need that*
  explained?'
—*'Shut up, Stefanie.'*
—*'Go on then, leave, go be an engineer.'*
—*'I can't 'cause I've no experience, which I can't get here*
and I can't bloody leave, I don't have the money.'
—*'And is that my fault? No. Go, go where it's sunny.'*
—*'If I thought for a minute, I could just move away*
without feeling guilty and burdened by you, I wouldn't stay.
I'd be gone in the morning but, no, you make sure,
that you're there crying, closing every door.'
—*'I can't believe your being such a prick,*
don't stay here for me, you stupid dick.

I am fine on my own, I don't need you!'

—'Come on now, we both know that's not true.

You're so neeeeeeedy, and you're driving me mad.'

—'I am not needy, Stephen, I am not that bad.

I just get these headaches and they're really sore.'

—'WELL, I CAN'T DO IT. ANY MORE!

I'm sorry,' he says, 'the way I've done it is wrong,

but it's over, I'm sorry, the love is gone.'

He picks up his jacket and walks out the front door.

I slide down the wall and sit on the floor.

I start to compose a text message to Steve,

—I'm sorry, I'm sorry. Please don't leave.

I delete the text, write the same thing again,

Delete it.

—You left your toothbrush.

Delete it.

—You're going to be the worst engineer ever. And I hope you are
    unemployed for the rest of your—

Delete it.

—I hope you can't get a visa because of that time you kicked
    the guard. And I hope someone in your family dies and you
    can't get a flight home for the funeral.

Delete it.

—Please come back, I think I'm going to faint. Will you bring
    me to the hospital?

Delete it.

—Come back. Please, Steve. I love you, I think.

Send.

It took Stephen three days to answer my text. My phone battery lasted for three whole days from lack of use. They say, 'When you don't use it, you lose it', don't they? Well, if they're talking about batteries, they're wrong. They're not talking about batteries though, are they? They're talking about muscles or brain cells or foreign languages. If you don't use them, you lose them. Batteries are different and so are people. These are the random thoughts I was distracting myself with when the text came in.

The first message came at 11 p.m. and it simply said, 'Are you all right?'

I didn't reply immediately. It was the tiniest amount of control that has ever gone to someone's head. *I will make him wait*, I thought. *Torture him a little, make him feel even worse.* And then just as I start to hate myself for being a cruel wench and start to realise that it's no wonder he left me, he rings. I answer too quickly and the hard-to-get-back game is up. Trying to get control again I clear my throat and say, 'Hi, who's this?'

'Have you already deleted my number?'

'No.' I decide the truth is the best option. 'I was just trying to be cool.'

'I miss you. I'm sorry for all the stuff I said.'

'I miss you as well – and I'm sorry too, I didn't mean to say I hoped someone died.'

'You didn't say that.'

'Well, I'm sorry for thinking it.'

'Do you wanna forget it all?' he says, and I can hear his smile.

'Yes, definitely. Definitely.'

'I'll be there in a while.'

Stephen with a *ph* is on his way.

I change the bedclothes and dump the ashtray that was once a litre tub of chocolate ice-cream. I get rid of the laundry by throwing it into the bottom of my wardrobe, use my sock to sweep the floor, then take off the sock and add it to the pile of shame in the bottom of the wardrobe. The doorbell rings and the pain is gone.

I am completely fine again, nothing is wrong.

That was the first fight.

It was awful and it felt like the world was ending. I had so many questions and things to say, and the idea of not getting the chance to get any answers was infuriating. The suddenness was the worst part. The instant change of state from 'in a relationship' to 'single' is too severe. It's like water going from vapour to ice without passing through the liquid phase. I need a good solid liquid phase to get me ready for any change. I just want to swim around in the liquid transformation for a while. Is that too much to ask?

The worst thing you can do to someone who hates change is give in to their manipulations to revert to the old ways. It looks like that's what they want, they want things to go back to the way they were and they will control you and manipulate you to go back there. But if you give in, that's more change, more inconsistency. You said we were broken up and now you are saying we aren't – WHAT GAME IS THAT?

This sends me, as a change-averse specimen, into orbit. You've now gone from ice to vapour again and I am floating around in steam molecules desperately trying not to evaporate. Stephen and I got back together, back into the steaming-hot vapour phase where the atoms, along with everything else, are unstable.

When we had our next fight, I assumed it would be the same – we would break up and get back together. But that's not how it went either. I've played this one over more times than the last … it's spun its way around my head and into a rhyming riddle I'll never crack.

This fight was different. He meant it. I could see it in his eyes and in how still he was. Unmoving. Like ice, not like steam. He'd got there before me. It made me wonder when he had decided to do it, because he seemed like a guy who was comfortable with the idea.

We had been at a going away party for Stephen's best and oldest friend, Ben. Ben was moving to Australia, to 'County Bondi', Ireland's thirty-third county. I'd been begging him for hours to go home because I could see that, as the night went on, the reality of losing his friend to the southern hemisphere was becoming real and, mixed with alcohol, was going to be a real issue within half a pint.

I stand up and leave without saying a word.
He follows me cursing, shouting something absurd.
I stood at the bottom of the hotel stairs,
people had followed us, myopic glares.
'I am not doing this here, let's go somewhere to talk.'
'Fine,' he says. 'Let's go for a walk.'

We didn't know where we were going, we just headed east.
We shouted and cried. We were talking at least.
'You know, Stefanie, sometimes I wish you'd just disappear
For both of our sakes, and I know that you'll hear
this the wrong way completely, and say it's outrageous
but your unhappiness is poison for you and it's contagious.
I wish I'd never even met you because I feel I'm stuck,
I love you but I wish I didn't give a fuck.
I find it too hard, too draining, too tight,
Jesus Christ, we can't keep having this fight.
I feel like you're choking me, fencing me in,
you're making me hate you, and I can't begin
to wonder what it's like to feel how you do
but I'm starting to not care about us, about you.
You need someone stronger than me
who can support you and be there unconditionally.
And at the moment, I'm not strong enough
to keep you and me from drowning. It's just too tough.'
At this stage, we've got to Sandymount Strand,
the tide is out and we walk on the sand.
The sun's coming up over Dún Laoghaire.
'Please don't leave me, Stephen.
(silence)
Did you hear me?'
'Ya,' he says, 'but I don't know what to say. I need to get out, to
    move away.'
'Stephen, please, no you don't. You're just sad 'cause of Ben,
but he'll be back, they all will, he'll come back again.'

'But why should he, y'know, come back to this hell?

When there's other places out there where he can work and do
    well

and earn a living, have a family, a house

not be offered cheese instead of money like a fucking mouse.

Why should I have to stay here and shoulder the blame?

If everyone's leaving, why would I stay?'

'Because if we all leave then we make it worse.'

He turns around, 'Open your purse.'

'What?' I say.

'Just do it, please.'

I open my wallet, he takes it from me.

'If you left now, this could be full

people pay you to do what you want, that's the pull.

There are places that want you

that need what you do,

but here you're just draining an empty pool.'

I can see in his eyes that he means it all.

Nothing I say can stop him or stall.

'You're going too, aren't you?' 'I have to,' he sighs.

'You should escape too.' 'I can't,' I reply.

'I don't want to be somewhere I don't belong

watching every Irish match and singing random songs

I wouldn't dream of singing if I was at home

but I'd just sing them there to feel less alone.'

The tide's coming in and my head is banging.

The alcohol's worn off and I am hanging.

'Can we go home, Stephen, I need to sleep.'

'I am going to go to my own home. To sleep.'
I looked at him for ages, and let go of his hand
And I just left him there, on Sandymount Strand.

I walked away with the vast expanse of water on my right. I wanted to run into the sea and never get out, to swim away from the whole situation. I'm always freezing though, so I had no intention of going near it. It took every bit of control I had not to look back. I imagined him standing there like a block of ice, frozen with resolve, me walking away as unstable as a steam molecule and the vast water between us.

They say that willpower is not an infinite resource. Apparently, you only have so much in a day. It's part of research into why people with eating disorders can starve themselves all day but then, when they start eating, all their willpower is gone. It's always one of the arguments of those people who wear the same clothes every day, high-powered CEO-types, they say that decision making and willpower are finite so they leave all of their reserves for big-picture stuff and don't get bogged down with minutiae.

I said above that it took all of my willpower and control not to look back at Stephen as I walked away from him. I wasn't joking. All of my reserves were gone because when I got home, eventually, I was buck wild. I had no more energy for composure. I stopped at a supermarket that had all of its yellow-sticker items freshly marked: God himself trying to comfort me. I bought a packet of sixteen teacakes, two chicken Kievs and an expired packet of garlic potato gratin. I had every intention of eating it all.

My housemates were up reading newspapers and watching music videos when I arrived. They could tell I had been crying and gave the situation the respect of their silence. I turned on the oven. And the washing machine. I sat in front of the spin cycle running the same questions over and over and over and over.

How had I lost him again? He can't leave and come back and then leave me again. I gave him everything, every part of me. He takes little pieces with him every time he leaves. When he's here, I know I'm his partner, his girlfriend. I know he likes two sugars in his tea even though he pretends that he only takes one. I know the beer he drinks. He keeps his toothbrush with the bristles facing away from the sink. I'm the only one who knows these little things. Until he teaches them to someone else.

I picked up my phone. Nothing from him. I started to write a message:

I know who I am when I'm with you, Stephen, but who am I now, if I'm anyone even?

I can't remember if I sent it. But I never heard from him again. I burned the top of the potato gratin. But I ate it anyway.

I thought he might ask to remain friends, because we were great buddies too. But is an ex asking you to stay friends after a break-up like kidnappers asking you to keep in touch after they finally let you go?

So, then I was single for a while. I've never done Tinder or internet dating but I have horror stories that match any episode of *Catfish* or *Deadliest Catch*. (I'm aware that *Deadliest Catch* is about courageous crab fishermen, but I think it would be the perfect title for some of the men I have dated.) Maybe all the normal guys were swiping right on Tinder and it was only the really, *really* desperate ones who were left on the streets.

I will share a quick example with you. I have changed his name to protect his pride. It's unfortunate he did not treat himself with the same compassion. Also, I hope I actually *have* changed his name. I can't fully remember and it would be just my luck to choose a fake name that is also his real name. Anyway, his name is changed or maybe it isn't. If he remembers mine he is unlikely to buy this book, and if he doesn't, he won't know I'm talking about him.

I met Brendan in a petrol station near the airport. The Boy Housemate had broken the kitchen table while the Girl Housemate and I were on holiday in Turkey. The Boy still hasn't admitted to what actually happened, but I suspect a house party was involved. I had to scour DoneDeal to try to find someone selling a similar table to protect ourselves from the small print of our tenancy agreement. I found a man selling one and we agreed to meet.

He was charming and inoffensive as he loaded the under-priced-for-its-value table into the boot of my car. I gave him the money in cash and we went our separate ways. Later that day, I received a text message from Brendan. I was worried I had given him a fake €50 note by accident. Images of court cases and evictions flashed before me. But, no. He was asking me out. I thought it was weird. I also thought if I ever wrote a book it would be a great little anecdote. And here we are.

I always knew Brendan wasn't going to be significant enough to get his own chapter but a few hundred words in a chapter about love is better than a night home alone, isn't it?

Brendan chose to bring me to a Chinese restaurant. This was his first mistake. Chinese, like? In 2014? It might have been striking in its non-nativeness back in the 1980s but the pervasiveness of the chicken ball has really taken the sheen off all things oriental in my eyes.

Having chosen MSG 'R' Us as the location for our meal, he then decided he would put the nail in the coffin that was our date by ordering for me. Those two things together were enough to justify me walking away, but I wanted to give his personality a chance to shine. Maybe you shouldn't judge a book by its taste buds. The third and final blow came in the form of a mispronunciation. I can cope with halitosis, I can cope with receding hairlines, I can cope with a family history of gout or Protestantism, but I cannot cope with the mispronunciation of basic words. If you tell me to be more *pacific* about this, I will gouge out my own eyes after I have stabbed you in yours.

I am not unreasonable with this boundary, however. If you struggle with my surname, that's OK. It could be pronounced *Price*-ner but I chose to pronounce it *Prize*-ner. If you struggle with uncommon words, that's grand – sure, so do I – but if you order an *expresso* or use the word *irregardless* or tell me, as one man did, that something is a 'blessing in the skies', I'm out. Gone. Over. Never to be seen again. I have been known to go either way with the mispronunciation of *Worcestershire*.

So this lad – Brendan, wasn't it? – offended me by ordering for me in a Chinese restaurant, then went on to mispronounce the order. It betrayed the fact that his palate had never had to deal with anything more exotic than a Dole pineapple slice. 'Yeah, we'll have number fifty-two please – the aromantic crispy duck.'

I couldn't help myself. 'It's *aromatic*.' Unless you're talking about this date which is a-romantic, as in the opposite of romantic. He talked about sports ball for the rest of the meal while I eroded the outer layer of my tongue and hard palate with prawn crackers, becalmed in the hopelessness of the evening.

I have experienced a great love. I have been more in love than I thought anyone ever could be in love – a love that gives Jack and Rose from *Titanic* a run for their money. I have woken up on cold mornings and been warmed by the feeling that I love and am loved. I have loved someone for the essence of who they are and not simply how they make me feel. I have had my breath taken away by the familiar-scented presence of him next to me. I have felt like I utterly belong in the easy sharing of an in-joke, I have felt joy and relief when he wakes up and sends a 'good morning' text message. That deep appreciation is something that will last long after the relationship ends. Which it did. That's life.

There are changes I can't control. But part of growing up is learning to live one day at a time. For future relationships, if they too must end, I wish for myself that the loss be a gradual tapering off, with lots of time to move from steamy love, to cool fluidity to the final ice-cold stage. The final ice-cold stage where I am on a floating door and he is in the sea, ice caked onto his nostrils as I slowly let him go and deny for eternity the fact that there was room for two of us on that floating door.

I think that's the only way I might cope.

10

IF RYANAIR DON'T FLY THERE IT'S NOT GOING TO WORK

YOU KNOW WHEN YOU KNOW. SOME FRIENDSHIPS are more than friendships but can't be because of outside circumstances. Like the roots of a hyacinth plant growing in the shape of the vessel that restricts it, sometimes relationships take the only shape they can.

In 2010, on the German border with France
in a hostel in Luxembourg starts 'the Romance'.
There were fourteen countries at the festival,
Greece, France, Belgium and all the … restival.
So to welcome us there, there's beer and wine
so we can get to know one another, relax, have a great time.
And after several bottles of Luxembourg's best,
bleary eyed, hiccupping, I do not protest
when a young Greek boy who I've been with all day
invites me to share some ouzo with him, how could I say,
No.
But I should have said,
No.
Said no to ouzo.

So we stayed up all night, on a Luxembourg couch,
smoking our native cigarettes until they ran out.
And then we walked in the half-light to a garage close by
and smoked new Luxembourg cigarettes under the sky.
And as we sat under German/French/Luxembourg stars
without the presence of German/French or Luxembourg cars,
just us in the silence at the top of a hill,
I sensed we were a slowly-falling-in-love Jack and Jill.

We talked together about what we want from the world,
our fears about living while our countries unfurl.
He's scared that he's wasting away living in Greece,
he craves small things for his life, not like world peace.
Like just having enough to always pay rent,

to enjoy his job and not eternally resent
his parents for bringing him into a world that's so grim,
that doesn't have enough time, money or interest in him.
And I tell him that I have similar fears
and I often wake up at night in tears
because I'm afraid of what's coming in the next few years.
And it was only a few hours but something occurred
and it wasn't all romantic and rosy and blurred.
Each of us knew when we went to bed that night
(alone) that something was the wrong side of right.

I woke up in the morning and stared at the hills,
I had that worry pain I get when I forget to pay bills.
When you know inside that you're in trouble
and ignoring it will only burst the bubble.
We had opened a floodgate with all of our chat
and now something would happen. I was sure of that.

Because I had a boyfriend at home, at the time
and things were rocky enough and, though that's not a crime,
acting on anything else would end it.
So I just laughed off the tension, pretended
I was in a happy relationship and things were class,
overlooking the fact that Stephen was a pain in the ass.
Calling me, texting, fifteen times a day,
'Why aren't u writing back? Can u just text to say hey?'
And I wished this love had been a just little bit blind.
There are all kinds of men, mine was the wrong kind.

And my time with the Greek boy was slipping out of my reach,
we spent our last hours together planning a holiday by the
    beach.
He said to come to Greece and he'd show me around,
we'd eat souvlaki, drink ouzo and walk around town.
At 5 a.m. when it's still buzzing, alive,
and we could take his parents' car the next day and go for a
    drive
to the nearest village where a blind man makes feta
and grows his own oregano, you can't get better.
Apparently.
And it was safe enough because we both knew it was a dream
and they don't always come true, cruel as it seems.

So on November fifteenth, at four in the morning,
under a German/French or Luxembourg awning,
we got on separate buses, tired and yawning.
Sat across from each other just a metre apart
with two windows between us, and I felt my heart
drive away with him on his bus,
wondering how I could make I into us.

Two days later, I'm back to reality.
Under a grey Dublin duvet of cloud and banality.
Saying no to a Metro with one in my hand,
crossing Millennium Walkway and that homeless man – grand.
And I get to my workplace, it's just a café,
stare at a blank screen, hours passing away.
When I sign in to Skype and staring at me

is the German/French/Luxembourg rose-tinted memory.
I answer his call and I know something's awry,
he's got a lump in his throat, trying not to cry.
He tells me his throat has closed up
and he has to force his lungs to breathe,
he broke up with his girlfriend, because of me.

'Sorry?' I say, and he tries to explain,
when you meet someone who's perfect, it can't be the same
being with anyone else, so you might as well not.
'She just wasn't you.' I felt like I'd been shot
in the heart with a blunt, rusty spoon,
something that ached as it entered and wouldn't heal anytime
    soon.

And though he said he knew we would never be,
because I was too far away and he had to stay in Greece,
he said there was no point in being with someone second best,
'If you can't be with your soul mate, fuck the rest.'

We met again in Belgium in 2011
in May and August, it was absolute heaven.
And then the following March, we met in Hyde Park
and sat for seven hours until it got dark.
Talking about why it was best just to leave it,
to stay friends but no more and just to believe it
would work as a friendship and not much more
'cause every time we said goodbye it was too painful, too sore.
And he reckoned the friendship would just give a padding

to the sharp edges of love, he continued by adding
that he wished things were different at the top of that hill
the night we were like a falling-in-love Jack and Jill.
He says the end of that poem is that Jack falls down
head over heels down the hill, he falls to the ground
and I say, 'But Jill tumbles after him and she doesn't complain,
she's head over heels for him too so they both feel the pain ... '

After two more platonic days being watched by Big Ben,
he walked me to Liverpool Street, hugged me and then
he walked away and disappeared into a Central Line train,
and I hated that public transport took him away again.

But before he left, he hugged me and held me for longer than
   friends,
and I know there's still something, but we'll just have to
   pretend.

11
LYING IN WEIGHT

YOU COULD SAY THAT THESE CHAPTERS, cumulatively, are about how I hate and feel I can't cope with most change. This chapter charts one of the most significant changes in my life and, as my nana would say, 'I've only myself to blame.' This decision I made to change, I made consciously and actively and it has had the most profound effect on my life.

In the eighteen months between February 2015 and August 2016, I changed my diet and lost half my body weight.

I had a moment one day where I caught myself in the reflection of a vacant retail unit on Grafton Street, and I didn't recognise myself. It was a gift. It was a rare opportunity to see yourself as others see you. The way the black contact in the store front had bubbled, the reflection was warped enough for me to think it was someone else, but not warped enough for me to maintain the lie that I didn't need to lose weight. I was eating four meals a day; I didn't drink but I spent just as much money on food as anyone in Copper's does on payday.

Up to that point, I hadn't thought about my weight – ever. I had always been overweight and people said I was 'big-boned' and that really had been enough to keep me from ever tackling it. I didn't think I ever *could be* thin, because I never *had* been thin.

I never knew the luxury of moderation. Moderation was as arcane a concept as I have ever known. Its lukewarmness as annoying as when you get a massage and can't quite figure out if they're actually making contact with your skin. Moderation is someone you constantly have to ask to speak up. It's tea that you've forgotten about and return to. It's the *or* in *all-or-nothing*. I don't get it. I can't see the enjoyment in it. There *is* no enjoyment in it. Moderation exists to keep everyone living in the middle section of a spirit level.

I need things to be black and white. I need one simple rule. I don't do balance and moderation. I can't count points or syns. I decided that a really simple way to lose weight would be to quit sugar. It's very simple. If an item of food contains sugar, I don't eat it. The same 'all or nothing' part of my brain that made me eat *all* the sugar is the same part that flipped and now eats none.

I was an overweight child, obese for most of my adolescence

and early twenties. As an overweight girl and woman, you learn your place in the world very quickly. You have to be a very good friend. You have to be loyal and always leave your phone on during the night. The night-time is when your thin friends have crises you must counsel them through. You must learn to give advice on things about which you have no experience. Hey, if priests can give marriage courses, I can advise you about how to win your boyfriend back from the girl he's been snatched by.

When you're fat, you must be funny. Witty is even better, but funny will do. If a conversation moves to food or looks or weight loss, you must get your self-deprecating joke in quickly before anyone else has a chance to think of it so that, when they *do* think of it, you can reassure yourself by telling yourself you invited them to think of it.

You must be 'one of the lads'. You must let boys and men believe you have no intention of ever even fancying them because they *obviously* don't fancy you so that would be awkward. All this, I learned and mastered. And then in 2015–2016, I lost 154 pounds, wrote my own TV show and was featured in every newspaper and magazine in the country. Women were now threatened by me, men were attracted to me and I had little idea or experience of how to be in this new world. It's a new insecurity.

Insecurity is a funny thing. Its effects are unpredictable.

I was walking down that same Grafton Street last September and it struck me that a group of girls ahead of me were all dressed as if they had come from different continents. One was in three-quarter-length sports leggings and a T-shirt. One was in a raincoat, scarf and jeans and the other was in a tracksuit and hoody. I was wearing a coat, but then I'm always wearing a coat (I'm permanently freezing).

In Ireland, your clothing is predominantly based on the time you choose to look out the window to check the weather. It's completely normal for it to be lashing rain and freezing in the morning which prompts the early-risers to dress in their rainproofs. After lunch, the sun has often burned off the mist and fog, and it can be quite bright and dry but still a bit nippy. The late risers can be seen around town free of the trappings of rainwear but still warm. Often in Ireland by four or five o'clock, it's absolutely roasting. Maybe it's the way we're tilted towards the sun and so far north but Irish evenings can be balmy, like. The shift workers or those with enough free time to do a costume change get to soak up the Vitamin D by wearing T-shirts.

Insecurity is just as unpredictable as Irish weather. It causes some people to turn into shrinking wallflowers, covered in layers and layers of protection against the rain and sleet or judgement or whatever it is they're afraid of. Insecurity made me hyperbolic. I became a superlative. I had to be the loud*est*, funn*iest*, best, *most* drunk, *most* memorable person in any given social situation. I wanted to be the favourite. When we had a substitute teacher or a summer camp leader or a coach, I wanted to be their pet. I wanted people's parents to think of me as the best friend for their child, the one they wanted as part of their family. Of course, parents are far more discerning than children and most of my friends' parents saw right through me.

As I aged, I became more subtle – or less subtle, but more adept. I would take social situations hostage. I was the one who had every chair facing them, holding forth with stories or songs or whatever I felt would hold the attention of the room. When people would tell me, 'You're so like this person or that person,' or say 'You remind me of x or y, you have to meet them', nothing was more sure to put someone in moral negative equity with me before I'd even met them. I had no interest in meeting someone who reminded someone else of me. I eschewed popularity competitions.

It all stemmed from insecurity. I was overweight and insecure. I was anxious that if I didn't stuff my overweight self into every quiet moment in a conversation someone else might fill it with a criticism of me. I was cruel to people who challenged me, excluding them or embarrassing them with weaponised intelligence. 'It's actually *espresso*. Not *expresso*.'

If you have always been thin, then you probably won't know the strange joys that come with weight loss. The little markers along the way that spark a light inside you and guide you to the next milestone. Being able to buy a pair of jeans for €8 in high-street shops, for example. All of my peers shopped in stores where the clothes are so cheap they are almost disposable. The mark-up on plus-size clothing is outrageous. Maybe it's because there is more material being used but I was never able to find jeans for less than €50 and they were no better or more durable than ones I have since bought for €8. One high-street store carried jeans up to size 20. I lost three stone before these fitted me. I bought a pair every three weeks as I dropped jeans sizes and although it seems so wasteful, I allowed myself to dispose of them as I went. After all, I had lived in the same tracksuit from the ages of fourteen to seventeen while all of my friends were keeping up with trends. Being able to buy cheap underwear – now, that *alone* is like the savings you see when you quit smoking. Although I support women in their fight for equal rights, I will admit I was SO DELIGHTED the first time I got wolf-whistled at on the street just last summer. I am learning to stand closer to people than I would have before because I take up less space. I am learning that being physically playful with male colleagues is no longer OK: I'm not 'one of the lads' anymore, rugby tackles are now seen as a come-on. And so on.

When someone would pick on me or insult me for how I looked, even if it was an innocent child who was just pointing out 'you're fat', I would absorb it. I would let it get me down for a while. Then I would pick myself up, brush myself off, pump my stomach full of sugar and complex carbohydrates and go back into the world. Being overweight is emotional armour. You're untouchable and so you can't be hurt. I think it stemmed from a desire for emotional numbness, from not wanting to access emotion. Either that or I just fucking love the taste of pizza. Eating sugar slowed things down when I needed things to be slow and digesting it sped me up enough to keep going. When you quit, you realise you have demons way deeper than donuts. It's an emotional crutch.

The first few days were difficult when I quit sugar. I had researched online how best to do it and had chosen the 'salt water flush method'. It was drastic, but the salt water that you drink with a litre of warm water kills the bacteria in your gut that feed off sugar. This avoids the flu-like symptoms that accompany the detox. Sugar-free and flooded with torrents of feelings, I would find myself walking around the kitchen in the evenings asking myself, 'What am I hungry for?' – and knowing it wasn't food. All change is difficult for me, but this was so quick and so drastic that it sometimes felt like a personal earthquake. I had stripped myself of my deepest and oldest coping mechanism.

Human beings respond incredibly well to incentives, and children, especially, are really incentivised by sugar. Recently, sugar has become the ultimate evil and its alternatives elevated to a godlike stature. So much so that sugar is now being taxed. When I was young, it was just a delicious thing to eat. At a young age, my brain, like the brains of most of my peers, was programmed to connect happiness and sweetness. If I did something good, I would get sugar. The instant gratification of sugar has changed how my generation process the world, down to how they watch TV and listen to music. On demand.

People's reaction has been intense.

'You look amazing.'

'You're so inspiring.'

'You're great.'

And the pressure makes me feel like my throat is going to close up. It's as if I have the eyes of the world on me and yet no one's at all.

It's a tricky situation because I'm not sure if I would prefer if they didn't comment. Some people haven't mentioned it at all, and that seems quite weird when we're together. It's like this massive thing that has happened that they won't acknowledge. One of my friends hasn't mentioned it because I think she feels that she herself needs to lose weight and maybe my change is difficult to watch. One man hasn't mentioned it because I think he feels that, in 2017, men shouldn't comment on how a woman looks, at all, ever, or they will be thrown to the wolves and castrated.

There's definitely a cohort of people who mention it because they think I want to talk about it. They are the same people who talk about the weather or whether you're going on any holidays this year. Their gentle questions are well-meaning and generally lubricate social situations. It's like conversational Sellotape for people who find themselves forced together for a while.

When people do mention it, I don't know how to respond. I think if I had to put a rule on it to keep things comfortable, it would be easiest if people made one positive comment that didn't warrant any response from me and then had their next conversation point lined up so we could move on swiftly.

I'm just tired of people asking me what I eat and then pausing for the specifics. I'm tired of people challenging me when I say I don't eat sugar. 'That's impossible. There's sugar in everything.' I'm tired of people telling me I can eat 'this thing they found in Tesco that has "sugar-free" written in pink on the front' and me having to explain that the terms *fructose, glucose, maltose, honey, agave, stevia, maple, coconut sugar, cane sugar, raw cane sugar* – all mean *sugar* and that I don't eat any of it.

The commentary and the compliments are so intense and confronting because they propagate the underlying message which is that thin people are somehow simply *better* than fat people. Every 'you look amazing' has a silent *now* tacked onto the end of it. It directly feeds into the insecurities fat people have.

It's the unspoken popular opinion that, 'You were unworthy, invalid, unattractive and invisible but now you've gone through a calorie-controlled redemption process, we accept you.'

I find myself, every time someone compliments me, feeling empathically attached to Sally Field. Her Oscar speech speaks to me from across the decades and I understand her words: 'You like me. Right now, you like me!'

But, from inside my head, the fear whispers to me, 'But you won't like me if I put it all back on.'

The pressure I feel to maintain how I look is immense.

People are definitely more fascinated by my weight loss than I am. That's unsurprising. I lived with it every day and saw each ounce burn away as I kicked and punched and sweated. It was a slow, steady change. For people who haven't seen me in years, it must be weird. Maybe it's this museum, voyeur, piqued-interest-in-strangeness that makes people want to look at before and after photos. But who benefits from those? Who would gain from a picture of me inside my old tracksuit pants holding out the waistband? It is the photographic representation of change, sure, but it also reinforces the idea that the small person I am is inherently better than my old fuller self.

Before all the press for *Can't Cope, Won't Cope*, I started working with a media trainer. I said to him, 'I've lost loads of weight and I don't want it to be mentioned in the press.'

He looked at me confused. He has since told me people have come to him with far less weight loss who wanted the very opposite. They request headlines and cover shoots and book deals because of their loss. I told him I wanted to be known for my work, for the quality and impact of my ideas and my ability to transfer them into the minds of other people. I did not want to be known as the ex-fat writer.

Because of how devastatingly good my media trainer is, I managed to avoid it coming out in any of the major media outlets in the country. I'm not going into the tactics I used, but I highly recommend Lorcan Nyhan if you ever need such help.

You might be wondering why, given that I've come this far without it being mentioned, I'm now divulging it in a book. It's a good question. I asked myself the same one over many sleepless nights. And it's because of those sleepless nights that I have to write about it.

I suppose I am trying to confront my fears. Maybe I think that if I give a bit of insight into this massive change, then people will have enough information to satiate their desire for answers from me. Maybe I see this chapter as a new form of protection against the future when I might not be thin. This chapter will exist and everyone will know that, at one time, for a period at least, I was thin. Maybe this chapter is just another permutation of my control freakishness. Maybe I'm trying to control how people talk about me and what facts they will have and use in the press. Is that bad?

When I do an interview – for TV or radio or a magazine or newspaper or online – I can't sleep the night before it goes live. I live in constant fear that *this* interviewer will be the one to deliver the cheap shot. *This* interviewer will be the one to dredge up the old photos and do the tacky before-and-after thing. And when one person does it, they'll all do it.

I have nightmares that I'll wake up one morning and find I'm fat again and no one recognises me, and when I tell them who I am and that they know me, they walk away. I have nightmares that tell me that if I put back on that weight one day, I'll be utterly insignificant and useless and irrelevant.

So what do I do when I wake up in the morning?

I weigh myself.

Weight fluctuates. But every time I am up a pound, I struggle to talk to myself and tell myself that it is impossible to put on a pound in one day, that I didn't eat the 3,500 calories it takes to gain a pound and, even if I have gained it, no one will notice or mind.

Before I lost weight, I lived in fear of the next comment. As I lose it, the fear remains the same. I'm starting to wonder if this is one of the things in life that will never change. People will always have opinions, and I will always be afraid of them.

As long as filters on Instagram and Snapchat accentuate your cheekbones, as long as magazines publish photos of people holding waistbands away from their bodies, as long as graphic designers pinch the silhouettes of models on catwalks in faraway places, there will be people who are afraid of how they look.

Weight loss is 80–90 per cent diet, depending on who you ask. If you asked me – after I sweated at you and had a panic attack about being spoken to – I would say 80 per cent. The other major aspect is exercise.

I hated exercise.

I used to take pride in telling people just how sedentary I was. I get bored of walking on machines and cycling but going nowhere. The only way I could exercise, when I was losing weight through sugar avoidance, was if I was tricked into it. I tricked myself by telling myself I was learning a new skill while also working up a sweat.

I started kickboxing. With all the passion I could conjure. Every punch landing on the bag with the weight of every insult hurled at me behind my back. Every feeble push-up burning the fat around my cells as my body screamed against the change.

I had never kept up any sport that was difficult. I don't know what drove me to stick to kickboxing. Probably the lack of judgement from my trainer, Eddie.

Every punch combination he taught me was a new way to handle the stress and anxiety of my life. Every painful two-minute skipping round taught me that even though things are hard and painful, they will end, they will not be forever. My body was learning how to react under stress. Just keep going, you'll get water at the end.

Every sparring match with my coach, which I inevitably lost, was fuelled by righteous indignation at all the comments I had absorbed growing up. My breathless kickboxing defeats compensated for my failure to say no to white bread. We moved on to kicks.

Every side-kick, attacking the times I had been side-stepped for a photograph. Every time I was told my headshot didn't need to accompany an article about me in a magazine because my 'face wouldn't sell print'. Sucking in my cheeks in headshots, aware of the camera angles that looked best but knowing the doubled-edged sword that if my photos looked good people would be underwhelmed by the real me.

Every upper cut stinging my knuckles.

Eddie told me that my hand muscles might be sore after the first few sessions; it takes a lot of effort to maintain a fist for an hour. I didn't feel a thing the day after. I was well used to remaining tight-fisted. White-knuckling my way through social events, trying not to see the people looking me up and down, the men turning away from me if they thought I was approaching, the disappointment in a passenger's face when they realised they had to sit next to me on a plane. Shadow-boxing in front of my own reflection in the mirror of the gym, throwing punches at the image of myself and watching it change over time.

Every jab-cross-roundhouse I sent hurtling towards my reflection cast off a painful memory of watching myself in mirrors of dressing rooms in shops I couldn't buy clothes in, waiting for my friends in changing rooms where I would sit until they stepped out to show me their many outfits and enlist me to choose.

I punch and kick at the old me because it's my way of keeping away what I don't want. I jump over the skipping rope with all the fervour of someone trying to outpace their past.

Over the months, kickboxing has changed for me. It's now my sanctuary. I feel about it the way my nana feels about Mass. I feel better for going.

Some days, I don't even train very hard. Some days my body is tired or I am stressed or sick. But I always go. Sometimes, I will gently stretch for forty-five minutes and do fifteen minutes of cardio. On tough days, I will sit with Eddie and just talk. We pick apart the complex webs of the world and sometimes that's much more strenuous than a high-intensity interval training set.

When I was overweight, the struggle was to become thin; now that I am, it's a similar but endless struggle to stay thin, to have the right clothes, to wear my hair the right way, to go to the gym, the list is as long as a treadmill minute.

When I was heavy, I didn't have the challenge of clothing. I went into a shop and the only criteria for purchase was that it fit me. Now it's different and I notice that I haven't developed in the same way as my friends who grew up thin. I haven't developed a taste in clothing. Other girls my age have tried so many shops and brands, they know what works, they know what they like. I don't, yet. I have to be severe with myself and remind myself in dressing rooms that just because the kimono fits me and looks great does not mean I should buy it.

Eating too much and not exercising wasn't just something

I did, it was who I was. I was very dismissive of people who were 'healthy'. I would upload photos of jumbo breakfast rolls with the hashtag 'clean eating' underneath just to highlight how stupid I thought it was. It was just insecurity. I needed people to know, by using the hashtag, that I was aware that 'clean eating' was a thing and was an option for me if I chose to get on board but I was openly scoffing at it while also scoffing five sausage rolls for €2. I was using my humour as a defence mechanism and whenever someone 'liked' a post where I poked fun at the idea of clean eating, I suppose I felt they were condoning my choices and giving me permission to continue.

I do believe, however, that there are dangers in people's new obsession with clean eating. People are beginning to see food as a sin. In fact, there is one particular dieting movement that calls food exactly that – they just spell it 'syn'. The trend of labelling foods as treats or cheats, sins or syns, perpetuates an underlying assumption that someone who eats a bag of chips is inherently less good than someone who eats raw broccoli, and that is going to make us see a major increase in people presenting with eating disorders. I think it's extremely treacherous that we now confuse weight with moral superiority.

Already a new phrase is moving into the public domain. 'Orthorexia' is the obsession with 'eating clean'. The sufferer has a compulsive desire to avoid foods they see as 'dirty' and moderation is discarded. It's like eating has become a new religion with vegan, vegetarian, gluten-free, sugar-free, dairy-free replacing priest, bishop, cardinal, deacon. The Paleo Pope sitting with his mitre at the top of the clean-eating food pyramid.

When I stopped eating sugar and changed my lifestyle, I quickly learned that I wasn't the bubbly, fun, life-and-soul-of-the-party person I thought I was. Without alcohol (which contains sugar) or a slice of cake in my hand or whatever it might be, I am naturally shy. I can't do small talk. I don't enjoy talking to strangers. I was angry because of all the years I had stopped myself from being the introvert I actually am, all the time I had spent trying to make my personality bigger than my body in an attempt to stop people noticing my weight. When I kickbox, I have a controlled way of releasing my anger. For years, I was an unexploded bomb, coating myself in lagging jackets of fat to protect myself from injustice.

I punched and kicked and sat-up and pushed-up and lifted and pressed and jabbed and skipped until sweating wasn't just something I did, it was who I was. I sweat *at* people.

I do it the way some people apologise – profusely.

It's almost always a cold sweat. One day, I had to interview a fairly intimidating public figure. I was researching a TV show I was writing. This woman is renowned in Ireland for being charismatic, powerful and perhaps a little intimidating. I hope to Christ she doesn't like to read personal essays by Irish girls in their twenties. If she does, there's no hope for me because unlike Brendan (of *aromantic* duck fame), this woman is bound to remember me. I made quite the impression on her the morning I sweated at her across the highly polished mahogany desk in her edificial office.

About halfway through my walk there that morning, an elderly American couple approached me and told me they had been mugged nearby and asked if I could help them. Dilemma. Maybe it's the German in me, but I think *anything* is more forgivable than being late. There is nothing more insulting than keeping someone waiting. It implicitly states that 'my time is more valuable than yours', and that is disrespectful. But I am also very compassionate and old people are my weakness. Of course, I helped them. I brought them to the GPO and handed them to that guard who is always standing there – I don't know why there is always a guard stationed outside the GPO, maybe it's in case some poor tourist's fingers get stuck in the bullet holes in the pillars. Anyway, my diversion delayed me.

I quickly weighed up my options and chose to sweat at someone rather than be late. I ran. I arrived with five minutes to spare, went to the bathroom, washed and blotted my face dry and then realised that that was a mistake. The water had opened my pores or something, and I couldn't stop the dampness. When I was eventually introduced to the woman (she was five minutes late), I greeted her with an apology. I'm lucky that she saw it as adorable. She petted my arm across the table and apologised for her tardiness. I could tell she felt the dampness of my sleeve. I didn't want to do anything that would betray my nervousness, so I left my hand there. She could use it like a cat's scratching post if she wanted to. She didn't touch it again.

I go to Eddie for one-on-one kickboxing classes twice a week. Outside of that, I walk to work every day and that is all. I don't run, I don't jog, I don't yoga, I don't spin, I don't Pilates (is that a verb?) and I definitely don't Zumba. I do the one-on-one thing because, even though it costs more, I don't like being in places where all the space is occupied by people who love to occupy space. Men with their protein bulging out of their Lycra. I grew up in a family where strong women were in the majority. I have never questioned the validity of my place in the world because I am a woman, except in a gym.

I've asked my closest friend if my weight loss was a big change for her. It might seem like a weird question, but I spent most of my time with this pal snacking on expired Easter eggs and chicken fillet rolls. She said the most striking thing was that, when I had lost a few kilos, I became really weird about being hugged or touched by anyone, perhaps because I no longer knew how much space I took up. I would stand remarkably far away from people in conversation, forgetting that I was now smaller and therefore less of an encroachment on their personal space. She said it was the same with slipping in between bins or poles when we spent time together in Manhattan. I would go the long way around something not realising that I could simply slip through the gap between obstacles. It strikes me now that that might be the reason why public spaces upset me. I've been told it takes a long time to get used to that sort of spatial change.

She also said there has been a marked difference in men looking at me. But I keep picking it up wrong. During that trip to Manhattan, we were in Whole Foods on Seventh Avenue, and I was walking around doing a small grocery shop. The security guard kept his eyes fastened to me the entire time. I felt so unnerved by it that I went up to him and indignantly demanded to know if he thought I was shoplifting or what his problem was. When he blushed and told me that he was looking at me because I was magnetic and he was going to ask me for my number, I was mortified. I just have no templates from my adolescence about how to deal with male attention.

I am now quite neurotic and obsessive about food. I'm always thinking about what and when I will eat. I am afraid that if I don't have it planned or controlled that all the healthy options in the world will disappear and I will be forced to snort raw cane sugar through a plastic straw off a bin on O'Connell Street.

My best pal says she's concerned that my fear of putting the weight back on is choking me. She would love to see me relax the control and develop a healthier relationship with weight and food. I think what people fail to understand is that it is terrifying. I tell myself that I would be just as valid and loved if I put every pound of it back on. That may be true of my family and my few friends. However, I know from how people behaved towards me in the past and how they behave now that it is not true of most. I also know from the press furore over *Can't Cope, Won't Cope* that looking like this has helped my career, and that's tough to reconcile because it proves that the world is more shallow than I believed.

Every chat show that has ever gone to air has, at one point, done a section about 'self-love'. Some expert is brought in to tell viewers that we should love ourselves just as we are. As a fat person, you take this to mean that you can continue eating too much and try to pretend that you are happy with how you look. If you took that advice to its extreme, you'd never get out of bed. If you only ever did what felt good, you would hit snooze and sleep until you got bed sores. Sometimes, loving yourself means pushing yourself far outside your comfort zone and making some of the biggest possible alterations to your life.

My friend did say, however, that my weight loss was great for her because she got loads of clothes out of it.

I look back at photos now, and then I look at myself and I wonder, is this who I am meant to be? Was I a thin person all along, just hidden under layers of adipocytes? Or have I lost Stefanie? The photos look like a different person to me, faded pages from the first draft of Stefanie Preissner.

I understand that sensation sells. I understand that the dramatic changes of Before and After shots, pregnancy photos, dyeing your hair white or getting reconstructive surgery are visually arresting. The contrast grabs us because it is simply so antithetically striking, but what we fail to realise when we gawk and ogle at these photographs is that we all used to be twelve inches long and now we are not. There is an absurdity to it if you imagine an article entitled 'Stars Before And After', filled with images of new-born Brad Pitt and then the grown adult man, because *that's* the biggest change.

I know that someone will take that cheap shot, probably soon. They will publish the Before and After photos. They will pretend they have done it in goodwill because 'they are proud' or 'it's such a massive transformation, you should be proud', and, depending on the day, I'll brush it off or spiral down to the pits of self-despair. Either way, it's out of my control.

12
WHATSAPPENING?

I HAD MY FIRST 'BEST FRIEND FOREVER' WHEN I WAS five.

He was named Brian and he never actually kept the Pogs he won from me. He let me play football even though I was a girl. He made sure I was aware of the dangers though. On the first day I asked to play with him, he picked up his ball cautiously and held it under his skinny arm.

'Do girls have groins?' he asked after several moments of deep contemplation.

I shrugged my shoulders.

'Go and ask my mam and come back.'

I ran into Brian's house. His back door was always open, the handle droopy and pathetic from years of small hands reaching up to pull it down. I shouted her name. She appeared, as always, in an apron with a phone trapped between her ear and her shoulder. Her chin jutted towards me and her eyebrows were raised: the universal gesture of 'permission to interrupt granted'.

'Brian wants to know if girls have groins.'

She smiled. One of those smiles that contained and held a laugh behind it, savouring the laugh for later. 'They do.'

'Thanks.'

I ran out the back door, swinging out of the door handle as I rounded the corner.

His mum was at the front door by the time I got around. 'But groins are not for playing with.'

I nodded and repeated the sentence the better to retain it. I ran up to Brian who was still in the same position on the green. A statue carved out of innocence and grazed knees. 'She says girls have groins too but they're not for playing with.'

'OK,' he said, satisfied. He handed me the ball. 'You can play, but you have to do stretches like me before you do or you'll hurt your groin and then you'll have to sit down to wee for a week.'

We shook our legs and pretended to do the hula hoop and the stretching was done. I kicked the ball farther than I was willing to chase it and went inside. Brian and I and our groins were friends for years.

My memories of my time with Brian are some of my happiest, but one sticks out as the first moment I felt real loss as a kid.

When we were eight we were in the kitchen of another friend who lived in the estate. Her mother was always baking and she smelled of Maxwell House. We were sitting at her green-tiled kitchen table when Brian came in to tell me his family were moving to Clonmel. I can still taste the tears in my scone.

I'm still friends with Brian after all these years. Granted, we aren't as close as we were, and he hasn't enquired about my groin since that day. There's a permanent space in your heart for your first best friend.

The Good Friday Agreement happened in 1998. I was ten. The tendrils of Protestant–Catholic tranquillity didn't quite make it as far as my classroom where tensions were building between me and the 'new girl', Jessica. She had the wrong pinafore and called our favourite band the *Space* Girls. My awareness of the Troubles in Northern Ireland was fortunately non-existent for my entire childhood. We would go on holidays to Spain and kids from the UK or Europe would say, 'Oh you're Irish! That must be really scary.' International media were reporting a war-torn island but the truth was, I had no notion where Belfast even was and was living a very safe, privileged life.

When I was ten, our teacher got sick midweek and a substitute teacher took over. The poor guy, straight out of teacher training and definitely no more than twenty-two. He decided a good thing to do, to run out the clock on his first day, was to give us a geography test.

Mr Walsh was the first male teacher I'd had. He was very skinny and his Adam's apple shook when he lost the sentence he was meant to be reading. That happened a lot. He looked like he was wearing the only tie he owned and the fold marks were still visible on his brand-new shirt.

He used to look into the crowd of ten-year-old girls with these scared puppy eyes pleading, begging us not to bully him, not to make some kind of joke. Sure, when you see that kind of weakness from a teacher, especially a male teacher … he hadn't a hope, like.

We didn't want to do the geography test, so we told Mr Walsh that every day on the dot of 12 noon it was school policy for us to say the Angelus.

His Adam's apple shook and he shuffled his feet and asked Jessica to start the Angelus. None of us had said the Angelus before. This was a stupid prank to get out of a geography test.

So Jessica started with the Our Father in her strong Belfast accent and none of us, including Mr Walsh, knew that there *is* no Our Father in the Angelus. She started off fine, grand, all normal, but when it got to the end, she added more lines! We all opened our devout eyes and looked at her. Mr Walsh looked at us to gauge what reaction he should have. She said, 'For thine is the kingdom, the power and the glory, now and forever.'

She opened her eyes. The whole class was looking at her, not going to let her get away with this mistake. It's wrong to say a prayer wrong. It's a sin.

I realise now, with my changed perspective, that this is how wars start.

'YOU'RE SAYING IT WRONG, JESSICA. STOP IT.'

'I'm not!'

'You are, you are! You're going to hell.'

'I'm not!'

Mr Walsh's Adam's apple was bouncing around his neck, his new grey shirt betraying his nerves. Sweat patches peeked out from under tense shoulders. Wearing grey? Rookie mistake. They don't teach you that in Mary-I.

'She is saying it wrong, sir. She's changing the line.'

'I'm not, sir. That's how the minister says it, it's fine.'

'The minister for what?' I pipe up.

'The minister at church. The minister for prayers.'

And the pictures of the Virgin Mary and the Sacred Heart on the wall of our classroom might as well have gone full Harry Potter and climbed out of their frames and appeared to us all, because at that point we all knew. Jessica was a Protestant.

'Sir, are there two ways of saying it maybe?'

'Yes, maybe, no, eh.' His feet shuffling like he's auditioning for *Riverdance*.

Mary pipes up from the back, 'Can we sing the national anthem instead?'

Panic flashes across Mr Walsh's young face. 'Eh, no, no, no, no.'

Mr Walsh skips through the lesson plan. On to the next thing. Geography. He tells us we've been learning the counties and can anyone tell him how many there are.

I shout 'thirty-two.'

Jessica calmly interjects with, 'There are twenty-six counties in Ireland.'

'There are twenty-six and six. DUH, Jessica,' Mary says.

Mary was the best at maths: twenty-six plus six is thirty-two.

Mr Walsh was very eager to move past this. 'Jessica is right. There are twenty-six and six, and the six are belonging to the United Kingdom.'

Jessica folded her arms in a smug, winning gesture. She glared at me.

'There's thirty-two too and they're all together, Jessica. LOOK at the map,' I say.

'Let us play Opposites,' he calls out, trying to distract us.

Looking back on it, our proper teacher had obviously left a note telling him what to do if we got rowdy. Our class were big fans of Ms Lucey's Opposite game.

'YAYYYY,' we all cried out, united in our love of distraction.

Here are the rules: The teacher shouts out a word and you put your hand up when you know the opposite of it.

Simple really. Harmless, even.

He gets his list of words. The religious division in the class is fading.

'Orange,' he shouts.

Two hands in the air.

He points at them both at the same time. This is a new move. Our teacher always does one at a time. We love the novelty of it.

Julie and Mary both shout, 'Apple!'

They both win, that's fair.

'Inside,' he shouts.

Five hands shoot up this time. He points at the twins to answer. 'Outside,' they shout, again they are both correct.

So far he's doing well to avoid any more fights. Class morale is getting higher.

'White.'

'Black.'

'Hot.'

'Cold.'

'Jill.'

'Jack.'

'Young.'

'Old.'

'Right,' Mr Walsh shouts out. He thinks he's on a roll.

Me and Jessica raise our hands. We look at each other competitively.

Mr Walsh tries not to sweat. Without pausing too long, he points at us both.

Jessica shouts, 'Wrong', and I shout, 'Left'.

We look at each other.

'It's left,' I say, my teeth clenched in my mouth.

'It's not, it's wrong, that's the opposite of *right*.'

'OK, girls. You are both correct, no need to get upset or argue. You both win.'

In hindsight, they're not wrong about generation snowflake. Everyone wins.

'Well, why don't you tell us which *right* you mean? Then we will know who is really right.'

I tell Mr Walsh that at a junction you can go right or left.

Jessica justifies her choice by piping up. 'Well, my dad says, "If you're not right-wing you're wrong-wing."'

'OK, girls, eh ...' He's sweating again. 'Let's watch *Aladdin*,' he croaks, and that makes us forget what's going on, and which one of us won. Watching the Arabic cartoon in a school run by nuns.

I learned a lot that day. Jessica stopped talking to me because I told her she wasn't saying the right prayer and that there were thirty-two counties in Ireland. She completely turned against me. When I got a Facebook account, she didn't even accept my friend request.

When our teacher finally did come back from being sick, she taught us that six counties belong to the UK. Jessica oozed with smugness. The teacher taught us the way to remember the six UK counties was with the mnemonic 'FAT DAD'.

The rest of that year, Jessica taunted me. She found a way to make sure I never forgot which counties were part of the Republic and which were not. She thought the best way to keep it in my memory was to make it really personal and bring it right home. To my home. Where I lived alone with my mother.

'Why are you so fat, Stefanie? Why do you not have a dad?'

'Fat Dad, Fat Dad, Fat Dad, Fat Dad, Fat Dad, Fat Dad', she and her friends would shout.

Fermanagh. Antrim. Tyrone. Derry. Armagh. Down. Fat Dad. That's how I remember. There aren't thirty-two counties. There are twenty-six and six.

Jessica invited everyone else to her birthday parties, but never me.

As a young woman, I was always told to be cautious of men. I was warned about behaviours that were unacceptable.

'If he says x, y, z to you, leave him.'

'If he won't take no for an answer, report him.'

'If he puts you down, show him the door.'

There was no grey area about which behaviours to tolerate and which to reject as unacceptable. As a twenty-eight-year-old woman, I can say with my hand on my heart that I have suffered more upset, more sleepless nights, more worry pains and more broken hearts – more trauma, frankly – from my female friends than I have from any man.

St Mary's Secondary School in Mallow is not the centre of the universe. But for the six years I was there, it felt like the old building with its mint-green walls and curvy skirting board had its own gravitational pull. I imagined the basketball courts and the old gym and the convent that loomed over the few acres had everything else imaginable orbiting around them in an eternal circle.

Like every other school that has probably ever existed, St Mary's was full of cliques. These little pockets of personality and poison. The teenage, oestrogen-riddled version of barbed wire, nail-filed just sharp enough to stop the Unchosen from getting in and the Chosen from getting out.

I was the overlap between the cliques. A go-between navigating the battlefield of bitchiness, flitting from one dress code and music taste to the next. Less like a social butterfly and more like Mowgli from *The Jungle Book*. Obliviously hopping between the wolf pack and the elephant herd not realising that anything outside of the animal family unit is prey. Apart from me, the borders of the cliques in St Mary's were fixed and fiercely guarded.

Gaggles of girls piled into classrooms where the walls sweated with their constant exhaling. We were corralled bulls at a rodeo. The pent-up oestrogen pulsing like adrenaline, so, at the very sight of a victim, they rush head first.

The victory, like at a rodeo, is lasting as long as you can survive in one of these groups.

I lasted sixteen years.

One of the groups I was part of was a coven of seven girls – eight including me, which they sometimes didn't. We called ourselves 'The Pals' because we had no imagination and the title fitted nicely at the top of the WhatsApp group. In the end, well, the end for me, we had become little more than merely a WhatsApp group.

When I started to make some changes in my life – losing weight, quitting sugar, and therefore alcohol – it seemed like those changes had ripples that ran through the group like little aftershocks, and sent each girl farther away from me in concentric circles. I tried to keep a hold of them by sending memes or dredging up old photos of us at school to get conversations going, but it seemed the past wasn't a strong enough glue to keep us together.

As with all groups, I was closer to some members than to others. I was closest to one girl. Let's call her Jane. Jane and I had been friends since primary school. (We made up after she claimed to have found the pubic hair in her garlic bread.) We were so close that her mother felt comfortable enough to give out to me. I felt like one of the family. I made an extra effort to see Jane even though we went to different universities and took different paths in life. We would have nights at each other's college accommodation where we would get take-away food, drink wine and scratch each other's backs. Literally.

One Saturday, I came back to Mallow because some of the other girls who had moved away were home. I texted the WhatsApp group to see if anyone was around to meet but no one responded. I scrolled back and realised I had been the only one contributing to the group for a few days. My screenshots and memes and funny memories had all been read but none had warranted a response, apparently. It was unprecedented. Usually that group made my phone sound like an eternal Angelus pinging away in my pocket.

I called up to Jane's house where I knew I was always welcome. She was there, in a tizzy, buried under a pile of copybooks and essays. I convinced her to take a break from her schoolwork corrections and go for a walk. We stopped by the river. She put her phone down between us. It pinged twice in a row. 'Sarah@ Stress Free Pals' and 'Catherine@Stress Free Pals'. I hadn't seen a notification saying 'Sarah@Pals' for weeks. I put two and two together and got a four-inch frog in my throat.

They'd set up a WhatsApp group without me.

I was being cyberbullied at the age of twenty-six.

I was devastated, and I can tell you that, since that day, I have thanked God more than once that social media was not prevalent when I was in school. The isolation and upset you can feel from people doing very little is crippling. If it upset me as a rational twenty-six-year-old, I am not in the least bit surprised that it causes tender teenagers to commit suicide.

They all apologised. They didn't mean it. They were stupid and they were so sorry and they really didn't mean to upset me.

But I had seen it, and I could never unsee it.

In the following days, each of the girls turned on one another, shifting the blame, hogging the blankets of innocence and exposing each other like shivering bodies in a bed of lies.

By bullying me – by creating a group whose very existence was just to exclude me – they forced me to scrutinise my relationship with each one of them. If you've never written a detailed pros and cons list about your closest friends, I suggest you try it. It's enlightening.

As we saw from *Friends*, though ('She's not Rachem', remember?), it doesn't often end well. After picking apart my friendships with these girls, I realised that, of the nine, only two of them were actual friendships. If I had met the other seven for the first time as an adult, we would certainly not be friends. We had nothing in common and because of the hurt they had caused, history was no longer enough to keep us together. Some of them tried to apologise, some of them didn't. History is like a joint bank account. It is sometimes the only reason two people stay together.

Either way, I am still friends with Jane. She had the courage to admit it all on that day. She showed me her contribution to the group was minimal and that she was uncomfortable with it from the get-go.

It's tough to spot the changes people go through during a lifetime while you're living through it with them. I went into that group and slotted into place. Over time, I didn't realise that the shape was stopping me from growing and from changing. It's weird to try to stay the same as you were when you were all fifteen. Being the same age as someone and from the same school catchment area might not be the best criteria for friendship.

It wasn't until I was in university that I had my first friendship that was based on mutual understanding.

In my second year, I worked as a lighting technician on the first-year production. During the performance on the opening night, I realised that one of the cast, Rachel, was looking very floppy and still in her chair. She was the only cast member in the show who was given a chair to sit in for the two-hour monologue showcase. Her cue to stand and deliver her speech was coming up and I was freaking out as it dawned on me that Rachel was fully asleep. The director was an absolute despot and would go mental if actors missed their cue.

I tried to work out a way to communicate with her on stage. The words of the monologue preceding hers faded away from my ears as I focused on a solution that wouldn't come. I decided I would take one for the team and play two seconds of a sound cue at the wrong time in the hope that it would wake her. Just as I was about to press Play, I noticed Rachel startle very gently in the chair. If you weren't watching her, it wouldn't have been noticeable at all. She made her cue. No fallout.

After the show, I approached Rachel in the green room of the theatre.

'Did you fall asleep during that show?'

She looked around to make sure no one else had heard. Then she burst out laughing. 'Please don't tell on me!'

I admired her honesty, her self-deprecation, her humility and the fact that she was inviting me to be complicit in her crime.

Since that night, Rachel has been my closest friend.

It's an unlikely pairing that always surprises the people who know us both separately. She is different and extremely similar to me, but with a curvier spine and fuller eyebrows. (That's not me being cryptic. She has a very curvy spine.)

A large part of our connection is fortified by our shared love of analysing other people. We play detective psychoanalysts for hours at a time and play out how we would live other people's lives differently. We're really good at nitpicking other people's relationships with others and themselves, but we're well aware it's a replacement activity for looking at our own shit. When we need to be called out on our own behaviour, we are always happy to do that for one another because we know it's coming from a place of love so it's harder to get angry or resentful.

I wreck her head, though. I know I do. Rachel is one of the most tolerant people I know. It's part of why it works. There are few friends who would tolerate me suggesting a holiday to Copenhagen to see a specific museum and, when we get there, choose instead to sit outside in the sun and work on my tan.

I was with Rachel the night my half-sister contacted me directly.

It was a Tuesday night. I remember because I was carrying two snack boxes and they were always two-for-one on a Tuesday. I stood outside Rachel's house with the two snack boxes. The music from the party inside was dimmed to just its bass notes through the front door. The drumsticks were getting cold in my arms while I banged on the door but no one could hear. I took out my phone to call Rachel to tell her I was outside and there was a message from an international mobile number sitting on my screen.

I opened it without examining the prefix. The prefix would have told me it was coming from Germany, and I know I would have left it until the following day in that case. It read:

> Hi. I'm Evi. Your sister. Our father is leaving my mother. Can we talk?

The words *our father* seemed to be in bold letters even though my phone didn't have that option.

So, yes, I have a half-sister.

I'd found out about her in a birthday card six years before this day. My birthday is in April but, in July, I'd received a birthday card that was blank on the inside. When I'd opened it a photo fell at my feet. Looking back at me was a child sitting at a table with a birthday cake in front of her. She was smiling at the camera and had a bow in her long blonde hair. The cake had eight candles in it. On the back written in black pen it just said, 'Your sister'. I had no idea how recently the photo had been taken. I had turned twelve that April so, at most, she was four years younger than me. I put the photo back in the card, put the card back in the envelope and never mentioned it to anyone again.

I thought about her infrequently for the following six years. If I was watching an episode of *Who Do You Think You Are?* or some such reality TV show that capitalises on the fallen branches of people's family trees, my mind would wander to her and what she might be doing.

I rang Rachel. She came outside and saw I had gone kind of pale. We sat on her doorstep and ate fried chicken. Rachel and I had spent a considerable part of our early friendship eating, while also talking about God and dads. She didn't know hers either and she was the first person who understood the duality of how formative and insignificant that was.

I talked to her about my fantasy of what this half-sister could mean. I teased out the holidays we would go on, the clothes we would share, the fights we would have, the 'big sister' role I would fit so comfortably into. We both knew our lives were not Disney films and, anyway, Disney princesses always had fathers, it was mothers they didn't have. At some point in the conversation, we cried together.

The biological sister didn't work out. She realised that my experience of being abandoned by our shared father didn't qualify me to counsel her through her loss, and she stopped getting in touch. But, in the process, Rachel had become my sibling. I don't think I've ever had a friend who wants to be around me as much as I want to be around them, except Rachel.

She is unchanging. She is permanent. She is like the Law

of Gravity, the speed of light in a vacuum, the value of pi in a Euclidean space.

I texted that line to her and she said, 'I'm not though. I change all the time, and so do you, pal. No one has changed more than you.'

I thought about that for a little while. She got frustrated because I 'left her on read' for ages before replying because I was thinking. She was right, you see. I have changed, and so has she, but in the midst of all of our changes, she has been there. No judgement, no molly-coddling, just love and a ferocious, unwavering, mutual loyalty. The steadfastness of my pal Rachel, the casual comfort of her and her curvy spine and her questionable dress sense is one thing in life I can be sure of.

Sometimes, it feels disrespectful to my connection with Rachel to merely call her a friend. That's not just an issue I have with that friendship. I think the word *friend* is offensively limiting at times. As I go through life, I have gathered around me people who are far more than friends. The connections are based on mutual understandings, similar or different views on the world, night-long discussions about our places in the world and generally an agreement that I am Beyoncé – always. They rise above those tenuous connections I had as a kid. Connections based on nothing more than age and geography.

How do you define friendship?
Is it the people you would invite to your wedding?

*Is it the people on Facebook whose posts you haven't hidden
    from your newsfeed?*
Is it the people whose phone numbers you have?
Is it the people whose birthdays you know?
Whose funeral you would attend?
Whose parents know your name?
Who know your childhood secrets?

When you are young, you can define a friend as 'someone who is the same age as you and from the same town'.

It's lovely to grow up and become slightly more exclusive and judicious. It's like Willy Wonka handing out Golden Tickets.

I have a couple of friends who are so close to me, they are like family. Describing them as 'friends' is like sacrilege. If one of them died, I would hate to think I would be lobbed into the mass of people who would climb out of the woodwork to call them *friend*.

I have one particular friend who is quite old. He has spent a significant amount of the past year in hospital. When he gets acutely sick, he tells the nurse I am his niece or some other relative because if I am demoted to the rank of *friend*, I am simply not seen as important enough to warrant a gown to visit him. He gives me that title to christen our connection with the status it deserves. I have also referred to him as my father or my uncle to slip past the next-of-kin brigade perched at the front entrance to the hospital. The title slides off the tongue with no stickiness as though it were a truth universally acknowledged. As if it were right and proper.

Since writing the above paragraph, two things have happened. My friend died and the zip in my wallet broke. They happened on the same day: 30 March 2017.

For the zip breaking, I blame the thickness of euro coins and my predilection for loyalty cards. Loyalty is one of the things I value most in the world. In fact, I would say it is the most important thing to me. I don't make friends easily. It's like I have a permanent 'No Vacancies' sign around my neck. However, when I do make a friend, I am fiercely loyal. I am the kind of friend who would give you the shirt off my back, even if you didn't want or need a shirt. I accept now that friendships expire and not all of them are meant to last forever but I feel buoyed by the fact that I am surrounded by great people. I have a family of non-family who will make sure that as I hand my shirt to the friend in front of me, another shirt – cotton and soft from years of washing – is placed over my shoulders by the friend behind me, as I am enveloped in mutual respect and appreciation.

There is nothing worse than injustices for whom there is no one to blame. I can't blame the thickness of euro coins or loyalty cards or anything else for the death of my friend. I can try – but it won't bring him back.

When you walked into the circular den in his home, where he watched sport and crime TV shows, you'd be forgiven for mistaking him for a piece of furniture. He was always still, but with a slow turn of the head and a curl of the lip, you knew you were welcome. The black leather recliner that had become his throne was placed in front of a bookcase bursting with well-thumbed tomes. When he spoke, in a hushed voice, I often wondered if he might somehow be hooked up to these books electronically – through the back of the chair maybe – because the knowledge and wisdom that came out of him during every conversation was encyclopaedic. Compendious though he was, I always felt he had all the time in the world to talk to me, in spite of the fact that there were always people in a digital queue for his wisdom and insight. His wife says I never knew him at his best, meeting him as I did in his last three sickly years. For me, these years must have been his half-life, a brief period during which he flourished before fading. He flourished in my eyes because I had never come across a man so brilliant. In his excellence, I discovered I was excellent too.

Our conversations were always warm – temperature-wise – and that suited us. We sat next to the wood-burning stove and I'd place my coffee cup up on it to keep it warm. That way I got to stay with him longer because you couldn't be expected to leave when your mug still had steam coming out of it.

It's so hard to imagine your life without someone in it. Until they're gone. Then it's the easiest thing in the whole world. They're just gone. I don't know why, but when I found out Tom had died, I immediately scanned my brain for the last time we had spoken and measured the distance from then until he died. It's like bringing a receipt with you to a shop to demand a refund because you are still within your fourteen-day rights to get your money back. I looked at the call log on my phone that proved I had spoken to him within hours of his passing as if time gave a fuck about my logic.

Because of my friend Tom, I have two pairs of leather gloves that I wear at the same time to keep my juvenile arthritic hands safe from the cold.

I have two songs and a poem that have a meaning they wouldn't otherwise have. That's three literary reasons to smile or cry depending on the day. Three reasons my life is more alive than it would have been if I hadn't met him. I have watched TV shows with him and got lost in their pixels with him, read books he penned or recommended and learned from their wisdom. I have felt an unparalleled sense of achievement from making him laugh out loud. He played hard-to-get with his laughter and, for the most part, even my wittiest remarks only induced a curl of the corner of his mouth. I stamped my mental laughter loyalty card every time I heard the faint chuckle and felt proud.

I have looked at myself differently in the mirror as I metabolise various compliments he gave me. I have memories that make me smile, secret unspoken memories that catch me when I remember, and those moments are stepping stones in a turbulent stream of grief. His life is like an oily handprint on the window of mine. Some days, I look past it, like my eyes looking past the end of my nose and not noticing. And some days, the tougher ones, all I can see is his big strong handprint on the window saying, 'I was here, and will always be.'

It hurts a bit more than a bit.

It seems profound now but, one day, he said something in passing that has stayed with me. He often did that, said something – casual, like – that would send your brain to work for days. This day, he said, 'Life is love and love is loss.'

And I know what he meant. He meant that I shouldn't try to

protect myself from the pain of grief by pushing everyone away. I can't force love to the margins of my life, thinking that will stop me feeling sad when the next person dies. He meant that if I do that, then my life won't be a life at all, and I may as well be dead. He meant that love is what makes a life a life. It's the thing that makes the small things big, the good things great and the funny hilarious. For him, it was the difference between the curl of his mouth and the laughter. It was so difficult to make him laugh and it made it all the sweeter. Love is the 3D goggles at the cinema that make the confusing image burst into brilliant, clear, vibrant life.

But love is also the thing that is going to hurt.

It's the thing that makes the rest of your days look like a bootleg, rip-off copy of a film, recorded under someone's jacket at the back of the dark cinema while they munch on popcorn. It's the shit version of a film you don't even really want to watch anymore but have heard you should because it's good. Some scenes are clearer than others but not watching it isn't an option.

I think about heaven now. It's hard to think about, because my friends and I don't talk about it. We've filed religion away in our childhood memories and we might fish it out again when we have to do some pre-marriage course or baptise our children to get them into a specific school. I think about heaven not because I am afraid of where I will go when I die, but because I don't want to believe the people I lose are extinct. And if I think about where they have gone, maybe that's enough to keep them alive.

My heaven would be the same pair of comfy jeans forever.

Jeans that never ripped or got too worn to wear. The same mascara that wouldn't be discontinued. The same people wearing the same perfume or cologne so I can identify them before I see them as they approach me for a hug. The same reruns of *Friends* and the same programme schedule. A constant stream of good coffee and endless dairy-free yoghurt.

I think about Tom's heaven, or if he even believed in one. Maybe it was the stash of iced caramels next to his recliner. Or the problems he could fix with his brilliant mind and cups of tea.

He kept a mental ledger of birthdays and anniversaries. A 'send flowers' list that would put any Google calendar to shame.

I never asked him. But as I saw his hermetic calm each time I visited, I often wondered if he was experiencing his heaven in life, and not waiting for death.

Maybe his heaven was beside his wife. His wife, sitting, reading, facing him and the fire and him looking beyond her at sport. Not talking, necessarily, but comforted by the casual presence of her love and devotion to him. He never got to the breaking point. Where teeth and joints beget prostheses. His heaven was the journey of getting there. To Ithaca. Wherever it is.

I wish I'd asked more about the hypotheticals. The *if*s and *what if*s of his beliefs. I could have bent my mind into the shape of his hypothetical. Even if it was just to find some comfort today, some solace in the belief that he is gone where he imagined he would go.

Looking at his grave a week after his death, I got the image of a boy who's just started in a new school and is wearing the wrong uniform on his first day. The mound is swollen and the flowers are doing a pathetic job at making him fit in amongst the other, flat, neat graves. Because he doesn't fit in. He doesn't belong there.

I would have loved to make him laugh more. My Tom-shaped laughter loyalty card isn't completed yet.

'Mind yourself,' he'd say.

I will, my friend.

13

MAY COPE, MIGHT COPE

AFTER THE AUSTRALIA DEBACLE, IT WASN'T A surprise to learn that I have social anxiety. I don't cope very well when I am in new situations or when there is any level of unpredictability. The combination of being in another country, away from my friends, touring a show and the vulnerability to public critique that goes with it, along with the social events and mandatory networking and socialising, were all just too much. You know the way people who have quit smoking for a time and return to it really feel the effects? After Australia, I took myself out of circulation online and in real life for a long time, and it seems my tolerance for social situations has dropped dramatically and the anxiety around it is getting worse.

The night *Can't Cope, Won't Cope* was first broadcast on RTÉ in September 2016, I was in a foetal curl in an armchair surrounded by my friends. I couldn't face anything that resembled a cast party. As I don't drink anymore and don't do crowds, I thought it best to stick with my inner circle. I considered whether or not my inner circle should include my 5,000 followers on Twitter. What if the people on Twitter hated it? What if they all hated the thing I had spent two years conceiving and birthing and raising and honing and polishing and preparing to present to the world? The anxiety was too much.

When I re-read that, I am struck by how narcissistic it may appear. Maybe I am narcissistic, but I think it's more truthful for me to admit that I care very much what people think. I always have.

I actively try not to care what people think of me, but it's a daily battle made harder by the constant validation I get from 'likes' on Twitter and Instagram. You can literally see how many people 'like' you when you upload part of your life online.

On the first night of *Can't Cope, Won't Cope*, I turned off my phone and watched through my fingers. I have this thing which I presume is not unique – very few things about me are unique, I think I even have the most common blood type – I *know* when I have done a good job or, more importantly, I know when I haven't. If I have done a good job, I admit it. If I haven't done a good job, then someone telling me I have will have absolutely no positive effect.

I was largely happy with *Can't Cope, Won't Cope*. I saw issues with it but for someone who hadn't written dialogue before, I thought it was a satisfactory first outing. I turned on my phone. The Twitter app had a red circle that popped up with a little 20+ symbol in it. My heart was pounding. I felt immediately so grievously sorry for every time I had taken to Twitter to complain about something.

I considered contacting Garth Brooks and apologising to him for being mean when he pulled out of the Croke Park gigs. I was tempted to get Ryan Tubridy's number and call him to apologise for criticising his choice of tie that one time. The tables had turned and the suspense and fear were overwhelming. I accepted a congratulatory call from my nana who was actually phoning to be reassured: 'That wasn't based on your life, was it? That was made up, wasn't it?'

'Yes, Nana. It's all made-up.' Eeeek. I hung up after the call and turned the phone back off. I wanted to enjoy my privacy for just one more night.

The following morning, I turned on my phone: 400+ notifications. A lot of them were new followers and new 'likes'. I read the tweets that had me tagged in them. Most of them were positive. In fact, because I am neurotic, I know the ratio exactly – 124 people sent me tweets about how much they had loved the show and how they related to it. One man tagged me in a tweet about how useless the show was. (I'm sure loads of other people took to Twitter to complain but this was the only tweet that landed onto my screen because I was tagged.)

And what sticks out? The 124 or the one?

That *one* negative tweet stayed with me the whole day. It sat up on my shoulder while I did interviews in radio stations around Dublin. It sat there whispering in my ear, telling me I wasn't perfect and someone out there didn't like me. It's my own issue that made me hone in on the negative and allowed it to erase the positive.

A friend of mine whipped me back into shape and told me to allow myself to feel the joy and the pride. Maybe it's that Irish fear of one day being accused of having 'notions'. God preserve me from ever having notions above my station.

My favourite thing to do is work. I love writing. I love my job. I love waking up at 4:30 in the morning when it is quiet and dark and my bed is warm and there are no distractions. I love turning on my electric blanket and my laptop and letting the words spill out of me uninterrupted by emails and texts and demands and enquiries. Then my housemates wake up – the Boy Housemate and the Girl Housemate – and we drink coffee and have breakfast and ease gently into the day.

I have a Fitbit watch. It tracks my steps. Because my job is so sedentary, I am pretty intense about getting exercise. I try to get 10,000 steps every day. It's a double-edged sword.

It makes me walk twice around shopping centres and take multiple trips to the sauce station at Nando's, bringing my fork and knife to the table on separate journeys. But it is also a saving grace. I believe if I didn't feel compelled to walk every day, I might never leave my house.

I feel like a little bee trapped under a pint glass.

I'm like a little flame. I get bigger when I am in my house. Then I go outside and I have to be an extrovert – and interacting with people just extinguishes me.

Meeting new people is OK because I meet them as I am now and they accept that. But meeting people I used to know is different. They can't reconcile the fact that I was once an extrovert and now I crumble at the prospect of conversation. And, of course, I understand that. They too fear the change. But people don't seem to accept when you tell them it's not about them, that they haven't done anything but that you just don't want to talk to them. They need a different answer.

The bottom line is clear to me. I am happier when I am not on any social media. But in this day and age of personal 'brands' and a focus on 'traction', it's virtually impossible not to be. It is possible, of course, but it would certainly have a negative impact on the 'reach' of my work. I weigh up the personal negatives against the professional positives and, as you can see from my online presence, the professional wins out for now.

I do sometimes take digital detox days where I don't engage with social media and I find it gives the little flame inside me the chance to get bigger and brighter again. Those detoxes manage my anxiety rather than cutting out Twitter and Instagram completely. I stay and manage now, rather than run away. I cope.

I find it scary how much the weight of people's opinions has changed. When I worked as a theatre actor, I think the biggest audience I ever played to was around 400 people. That's a large theatre audience, but you can still see the whites of their eyes. You can see when the older lady with the scarf is getting a bit bored, when she starts shuffling, and you can adapt your performance to give your attention to her and keep her engaged. Now that I write for television, I am projecting my thoughts and ideas into people's living rooms. The people who now view my work haven't bought tickets to see my show, they aren't invested in me, and there's always the chance that they will see my presence in their living room as trespassing somehow.

With the advent of Twitter and other social media, this angry person who takes issue with the fact that my show has been beamed into their house has the same platform as a professional television critic. Just like the man who is unhappy with the temperature of the tomato slice in his ham and cheese toastie and takes to TripAdvisor to scorn the restaurant that served it, the humble opinion has been elevated to a heightened impact level. Joe Bloggs has the same power to close a restaurant as a top-class restaurant critic. That's a massive change, not just for me, but for society in general. We are more vulnerable than ever to the whims and tastes of the general public – and that is scary.

14

IT'S ALL GRAVY

MY MOTHER IS A PHENOMENAL COOK. SHE HAS
rows and rows of cookbooks. You can tell straight away which
recipes are her favourites because those pages are speckled with
tomato sauce or dabbed in flour or have tiny specs of flaked food
on them. Each caked-on ingredient is a timeless endorsement
of her approval.

When I was growing up, my friends would always hang on
well into the evening in the hopes of being invited to stay for
dinner, which they always were. Because of my discomfort with
surprises and my love of routine, the week's menu was decided

in advance and rarely strayed. Spaghetti Bolognese, lasagne, lamb chops with chips and coleslaw, tacos, and brown stew were personal favourites. Each one was made from scratch with a recipe other mothers could never replicate. Other mothers were always disappointed when their brown stew didn't ignite the same excitement in me. When I saw the floating celery bobbing around the bowl in front of me, I just knew their hearts weren't in it like my mam's was.

I hated being at one friend's house on a Friday. 'White Fridays' was a term I invented and kept to myself so as not to seem critical of the very pale plate that was laid in front of me on a Friday at her house: white fish, mashed potatoes and cauliflower.

One tradition that never ever changed was a roast dinner on a Sunday. Chicken, beef or lamb with roast potatoes and some vegetable that was eaten first just to get it out of the way. All of this was drowned in my mother's gravy. My neighbour was extremely fond of my mother's cooking and her name was eventually added to the pot on a daily basis. She always talked about my mother's gravy. My mother would joke, calling it a 'secret recipe', without ever actually telling her what it was or how to make it.

I knew my mother was a fabulous cook and I made no apologies for telling friends and teachers this fact. Regional Ireland has a way of elevating people to celebrity status for things like how they cook a ham or how they bake an apple tart. Mallow is no different.

One Sunday, I watched my mother cooking. Our kitchen was

small and I was always under her feet so I had never observed the hard labour involved in preparing a roast dinner from scratch.

As all of the trappings were brought to the table, I watched the button on the kettle click off and the steam rise and sweat off the tiles in the kitchen. Then I watched, almost in a daydream, as my mother opened the corner press. The right-hand part of the door moved at the hinges, pulling the left door panel back to reveal a trove of jars and cans. Spices and soups, chutneys and relishes, a whole host of pots my palate was not yet ready for. I watched in awe as she reached for a brown cardboard jar: 'Erin Gravy Rich', it read. She grabbed a Pyrex jug, quickly scooped two heaped teaspoons of brown powder in and added the steaming hot water from the kettle. As she stirred and stirred, as the powder swirled and turned more viscous, as the water turned from clear to murky, my mind did the opposite.

My mother didn't have a gravy recipe.

My mother was making gravy from a jar.

My Michelin star mother was … imperfect.

Now, she had never lied. She had never claimed that the gravy was home-made. She had only referred to the recipe as a 'secret'. So I couldn't even throw the accusation of liar at her.

That was the day I realised that adults aren't perfect, they take shortcuts and they don't have all the answers. I won't lie, for the first time ever on that Sunday, I didn't finish my dinner. I let the potatoes and half a chicken leg sit in the brown-liquid reality that my mother was not a superhero chef. I think I got over it by about 8.30 p.m. when my stomach rumbled and the theme tune to *Glenroe* threatened to bring the weekend to an end.

My mother didn't ask to be elevated to the level of culinary demigod. I painted her into piquant perfection, without any request from her to be put on a pedestal from which she would inevitably fall. It seems that's just something kids do to the adults who influence them. It's the most dangerous part of the mentor–neophyte relationship and leads to clichés like 'Do as I say, not as I do' ending up on fridge magnets in family homes across the land.

15

LOTS OF
SMALL CHANGE

THIS CHAPTER COMES WITH A HEALTH WARNING. I feel like an old codger sitting in the corner of a room speaking in sentences that start only with 'In my day', and pointing out everything that has changed. This is not the case. I'm not whining that no one appreciates the abacus anymore. I welcome the continued technological addition of the scientific calculator to my phone. It's incredibly useful to be able to work out the Sin, Cos and Tan of the price of groceries while I'm ambling around the supermarket. Just as much as the next guy, I love the tools modernity has invented to help me with my life. I mean, where would I be without the gadget that separates my egg whites from my egg yolks? I bet Palaeolithic man would have been intrigued to know how many steps he took in a day and how many calories he burned while chasing wildebeest.

There is no doubt that we have come a long way since hunter-gatherer times. Little changes can be so simple they go unnoticed. When some person in a science lab invented the first hints of an internal modem, it didn't make headline news. Progress is made behind the scenes and it's the end product that benefits us. In that way, the changes happen much more slowly and steadily than they seem to. When you look back and see how things have changed in the twenty-eight years I have been alive, altogether, it's much more dramatic.

I have been to Australia once more since I was there on tour with *Solpadeine Is My Boyfriend*. In Brisbane, the hotel I stayed in was right on the river with a walkway along the whole riverbank lined with exercise equipment, coffee stalls, cycle lanes and the most fascinating shaped trees I've ever seen. In Australia, trees are permitted. Branches grow parallel to the ground and then rise up whenever they feel like it. The roots are facilitated by the concrete around them, given space to breathe and this all makes for some pretty impressive urban landscaping.

The evenings get dark early in Queensland, but it's still warm and an ecological twilight orchestra plays the loudest chorus out of the grass, trees, bushes and anywhere green. I can identify crickets, I can identify cane toads (and steer well clear) but one ubiquitous sound I couldn't identify, so, in my infinite search for answers, I went looking. My search took me into a tree.

I scaled the tree with blind faith and bold precision, never stopping to think, 'How the hell am I gonna get down from here?' At the crest of a branch hanging over a creek, I was reminded of the day the town council cut all of the bottom branches off the trees around my primary school in a benighted attempt to protect us from falling. We tripped over each other and cut our knees watching the arborists amputating limbs from our favourite tree as we walked to the playground. That was the year before they banned running in the yard. It was also the year, incidentally, I started gaining the weight it would take me two decades to lose.

They only had to fell one branch from each tree to make them completely obsolete as climbers. Simple and devastating. It's clever, really, because you only have to make the first step of something intrinsically difficult to make the entire journey impossible.

In quiet protest against the great injustice my friends and I were experiencing, I took it upon myself to find a solution. In my friend's father's shed, we found an old bed. We emancipated the slats from the base and leaned them against a wall, kicking them at their weakest point to break them into pieces we could conceal in our schoolbags. We also took a hammer and some nails and, the following Monday, drove the nails through pieces of 'borrowed' wood that lay horizontally across the lower part of the tree to form a makeshift ladder. In today's terms, I was leveraging the wood to gain leverage among my peers. Back then I was just 'sound'. Immediately, the caretaker removed the slats, wrapped us all in cotton wool and changed how we would experience childhood.

We stopped making judgements about which trees were safe.
We stopped assessing how high was too high.
We stopped standing at the bottom waiting to catch our friend if
  they fell.
We forgot how to give someone a 'leg-up'.
We forgot how to be playfully competitive.
We forgot that there are consequences and you always have to
  consider your way back down.
We forgot that it's OK to fall and, in that, we forgot how to
  manage our own failure.
Why? Because of the fear of litigation.

The fear that if we fell and hurt ourselves, our overprotective parents would need someone to blame. The fear that we, unlike every human being since the dawn of humanity, would not survive a fall from a tree or a broken limb. The fear, perhaps, that young people, by challenging themselves against nature, were learning how to assess risk too well and might be dangerous businesspeople in the future. But mainly because they didn't want the responsibility of it.

When we asked the teachers we got a one-word reply: 'Insurance.'

And so I changed the name of my favourite game from 'hide

and seek' to 'health and safety' and, because of the level playing field and no chance for elevation, I was always caught.

Slowly, as the Celtic Tiger started his terrible purr, birthday parties started to go 'off-site'. All of a sudden we were allowed to climb walls with plastic rocks drilled into them, attached to harnesses and hanging over a spongy floor. The activity was undertaken in forty-minute slots with the birthday boy getting to wear an elaborate helmet, and when we had all climbed up and down the wall once, we were unstrapped and stuffed with pizza.

In seeking perspective and a break from the noise and chaos of our prepubescent hormones, we were forced to find other ways of getting high. Eventually.

Maybe they wanted to protect us. Maybe they didn't want to deal with our inevitable hurt. Maybe it was inevitable. Maybe when all of nature is free and there's no one to sue, only then can we have our childhoods back. That seems a bit dramatic, though. I have also learned that in some places it is now not only illegal to climb trees but also to play with conkers: another favourite past-time of mine that taught me how to discern fresh from stale, taught me aim and dexterity, and how, generally, the best things are never thrown on the ground.

What's next to be stricken from the list of permitted childhood activities?

Making a daisy chain? Rolling down a hill? Making boats out of milk cartons? Jumping in puddles? Pushing people into swimming pools? Riding bikes? Jumping for hopscotch? Doing *anything* with a skipping rope?

If you have an entrepreneurial eye and an iPad, however, you could do worse than design an app that simulates all of the above. There's an idea with roots.

With the progress being made in technology, things are changing, adapting and rocketing away from the way they were only a few years ago. Walking around my neighbourhood in north Dublin, you don't see bikes left leaning casually against the walls when kids visit their friends' houses. I remember consulting my group of friends when we were about thirteen because we were getting bikes for Christmas and we needed to make sure they were all different. The bike shop in Mallow only had so many types but, because we all hung out together, seven, eight or nine bikes would be strewn across a lawn in someone's front yard, so identifiers were crucial. I've seen bikes in Dublin city centre with three padlocks on. The frame of the bike ends up looking like that bridge in Paris where lovers go when they feel insecure about their relationship. They believe that buying a €3 lock from a man selling them for €15 and locking it to a bridge, throwing the key into the Seine, will ensure neither of them is ever unfaithful or no longer interested.

Bikes wrapped in chains and padlocks aren't the only changes that strike me in my daily life.

Below is a list of things that I didn't notice had changed until I was confronted with the past.

1. The internet

I recently found myself in a cotton field in Abilene, Texas. The rental car we were driving was parked close by and, apart from it and the two colleagues who were travelling with me, there was nothing else, except cotton, as far as I could see. Taking out my phone, I quickly found myself in the opening scene of a horror film. You know that moment where the protagonists realise there is no phone signal? (In defence of horror cinema, they have it super-tough now trying to create legitimate reasons for future-corpses to find themselves unable to call, tweet, text, email for help.) For any aspiring horror film writers reading this, I can recommend Route 277 from Abilene to Wichita Falls for the setting of your film because there is no hope of ever being found. We didn't know what direction we were meant to be going. None of us could navigate using the sun or any other celestial bodies and so we were completely technology-dependent. We couldn't source the number of the hotel, load a map, ask Siri or do any of the things we have become so used to doing. It struck me that this wouldn't have happened in the 1990s. We would either have had a map, saved the number or at least allowed ourselves the time to get lost rather than leaving the bare 149 minutes that Google had told us the journey would take.

2. Cameras

There's an indigenous population somewhere who believe that when you take their picture, a piece of their soul is captured and trapped in the photograph and they are less complete than before the snap was taken. If this is true, then I am walking around like the half-dead and any child born in the last three to six years is a zombie before their umbilical stub has turned black and fallen off.

Piles and piles of sepia-toned memories of my childhood are packed into photo albums and drawers in the houses of my relatives. The hard-copy photograph means there is less of a threat of them being shared online but they still exist to haunt me. I don't think people should be allowed to take any photos of you from the ages of six months until puberty has passed and your hormones are not ricocheting around your body like a ping-pong ball in a tumble dryer.

Kids nowadays can watch themselves age in real time as though their life were a stop-go entry to a short-film festival. I am guilty of it too. When I spend time with kids, I feel the need to take photos of them and post photos of us on Instagram. Perhaps I'm trying to prove to future husbands or adoption agencies that people trust me with their offspring?

On the plus side, no one will be subjected to a collection of holiday photographs half-disguised by a thumb ever again.

3. Doorbells

I feel guilty when the statistics come in each January and a news anchor reports that retailers have seen *another* decline in pre-Christmas sales. The guilt is uncomfortable but not strong enough to stop me shopping online. I love online shopping. I rarely actually purchase but, every day, I go on to the same sites to see if anything has changed. If I get stuck in a scene that I am writing, I wander over to look at shoes or jeans and all of a sudden it's two hours later and I still have no idea how to resolve the narrative dilemma I am in.

The only thing that puts me off ordering online is the delivery part. We don't have a doorbell. We took it off the wall next to the front door. When I was young, and being an only child, I was often lonely or bored. The reverb of the 'ding dong' wouldn't have stopped before I was on my feet screaming that I would get it. Now, that same sound sends a chill through me. Who the hell is at the door? When I hear a doorbell, I immediately check my phone. It isn't that I have mistaken the sounds, it's that, if someone is at my door and hasn't texted or called to say they are, then I have no intention of answering it.

So unemployed is the humble doorbell now that my nana has a note on her doorbell that actually instructs people how it should be used: 'Press at least twice and wait.' She deems it necessary to leave the note because it takes her ages to get all the way to the door and people have become impatient.

All the grandchildren in my family get stuff delivered to Nana's house because someone is always there. It's insightful then that we still get notes from delivery companies that passive-aggressively say, 'Sorry We Missed You.' We thought the delivery drivers just weren't seeing the note or Nana didn't hear the bell. One day, I was looking out the upstairs window when I saw the real reason we were having to drive to some sorting office in a faraway industrial estate to make the Spring/Summer Collection collection.

Delivery men have become so accustomed to being ignored at the door that they don't even try. If you're not there waiting for them, they drive away. This driver hopped out of his van with the 'Sorry We Missed You' note and popped it straight in the letterbox without even trying.

I want to say for the record that I *do* have a TV licence. I doubt I will ever have to prove it, though, because I will never answer the door. I have heard that the inspectors stand near the house and wait for you to come or go so they can ask you in person. When that day comes, I will wave my licence with pride from my doorstep.

It's definitely not only my housemates and I who freeze on the couch when the doorbell shatters the illusion of privacy. Look at the recent census campaign. They had to *advertise* on TV, radio and in print that the census man would be coming just so people would answer the door.

I will never understand those households that have those doors that are always open. Where people just walk in. What kind of madness is that?

4. Music consumption

I wasn't part of the generation that sat in front of a wireless. Nor was I in my room with my youthful fingers poised over the record button on a cassette player ready to catch the Top 20 hits of the week. I was part of generation Napster (which was not invented by Justin Timberlake, contrary to popular cinema).

My friends and I would download music illegally and put it on CDs for each other. The thing with Napster was that you had to download it, so it took up a lot of space on your tiny hard drive. You also had to know exactly what you were looking for. Once downloaded, it was yours. Today, music is transient. With Spotify and YouTube, Vevo and Tidal, it's like listening to someone else's mix tape, something I never enjoyed.

You know when you scroll through someone else's iPod, or even their phone, and you see how, even though the device in your hand is the same, the apps are laid out differently from yours, the songs on their playlists are different and it all feels weird and discomfiting? That's how I feel when I listen to Spotify. The open access to music, music channels, music videos and digital music sites has made music less appreciated. Can you imagine what it must have been like to experience music back when Mozart and the lads were composing? Imagine how you might appreciate an aria if you knew you would never hear it again. Imagine how delicious it would be to go to a concert hall and listen to an orchestra when there was nowhere else you would ever hear music, from one end of the year to the next. That must have been magical.

5. Pregnancy

Watching TV with the Boy Housemate and the Girl Housemate is always interesting. Different tastes. The Boy Housemate will almost certainly opt for Netflix, which feels like too much of a commitment for me. There's too much choice. The Girl Housemate will opt for music videos but usually won't go to YouTube on the Smart TV. She prefers Music Television. My preference is always an Irish TV channel, ideally a chat show, current affairs programme, a quiz show or a documentary. I am the first up in our house, so morning TV is dictated by me and then it switches.

One evening, I arrived home and the Girl Housemate had MTV on in the background while she worked on her laptop on the couch. Seeing that she wasn't paying attention, I asked if I could switch from *Teen Mom* to my favourite Irish TV channel. When I did, the film *The Magdalene Sisters* was on. Unable for that level of emotion on a Tuesday evening, I handed the remote to the Boy Housemate, who put on Netflix.

The contrast in the two shows started a discussion about how teenage pregnancy has changed dramatically in recent history. Being young and pregnant now doesn't mean you get sent to the nuns and forced to wash clothes. It's more likely to mean you get shipped off to MTV to try to capitalise on the unplanned event.

We still have a ways to go regarding unplanned pregnancy in Ireland, though – some things haven't changed at all and they need to.

6. Mobile phones and egos

I was having a disagreement with a relative over the phone last December. I've never had a run-in with any of my family. It was right out of left field and caught me completely off-guard. I was shaking from the frustration and the fright so much that, as I was hanging up the phone I dropped it. Bam. Brand-new pieces of iPhone 7 and insufficiently robust iPhone 7 cover shimmered on the footpath like glitter on liquorice. There was a time when you would almost feel safe walking home at night with your phone in your pocket. Not because you could easily dial for help but because the early mobiles were so brick-like that they served as a weapon.

During the argument, my relative had insulted me greatly

with her accusations. My ego was damaged. *Was I always so fragile?* I thought, as I called my mother from my friend's phone and sobbed about my broken screen.

The penalties for many small offenses, like breaking your phone, have grown to extortionate amounts. It's cheaper to drop yourself off a wall and break your arm, incurring a medical bill from an A&E trip and the follow-up x-ray and plaster cast than it is to drop your phone from your hand and pay to get the screen fixed.

7. Dating

We all know that, back in the day, men asked ladies to dance and then organised to meet them at a specific time and location and showed up without any further confirmations being necessary. We also all know that this has changed dramatically. However, it's not just the reliability that has changed. In the short time I have been alive, the process of dating has become as unrecognisable as an internet troll and their profile photo.

It's always been a bit of an effort. You had to find out what pub someone was going to be in or what hobby they liked so you too could take it up and find reasons to be in their orbit. I know a guy who joined my youth theatre just because he fancied a girl who went there. He went on to become a fine and established actor.

Nowadays, you don't have to be on the same continent, speak the same language, have the same interests or even be the same classification of organism as someone to find a date. Thank you, internet dating.

This is one of the major changes of the twenty-first century and has completely eroded the romantic stories of 'how people met'. It started with internet chatrooms, which still required you to have some form of a meet-cute because not everyone there was looking for a partner. Now, dating sites provide the fictional fishing rod for hopeful singles to cast into the ocean at one another.

It's a minefield.

Before, the question bandied between girl friends of 'Does he like me, I can't tell?' was as complicated as it got. Now, I find myself chatting to my friends as we try to work out if guys online are looking for a date or for our bank details. Do they just want a hook-up or are they looking to get serious? The questions are never-ending. If I tell them I am looking for something more serious is that a turn-off? When do I let them know that I don't drink? When do I let them know I am from Cork? Which is worse?

I have never gone on an internet date but, if I did, I would make sure to ask what the name of their first pet was *and* what their mother's maiden name is. I'd just casually drop it into the small talk. That way, when it ends, I have the answers to the verification questions for most of their online stuff and I can get my revenge – if revenge is needed.

8. Cats

OK, the biological make-up of cats has not changed significantly in my twenty-eight years on this planet. Cats have not gone through any major evolutionary change. I do feel though that they have really come into their own in the past few years in some sort of feline fifteen minutes of fame.

I am asthmatic, so I've never been fond of cats. Because they tried to kill me several times with their dander, my hatred is justified. When I was a kid, however, they were simply humble domestic house pets. They were also the subject of Hallowe'en presentiments and superstitious cautions that bordered on racist in their colour bias. Now, they're an internet sensation. People watch videos of cats more than anything else. They have been revolutionised and monetised within an inch of their nine lives. There isn't a person with internet access who doesn't see a cat photo or meme at least once a day.

9. Sweets

My favourite M&Ms were always the blue ones. My favourite Mr Freeze ice-pops were also the blue ones. I think I liked that the stain on my tongue and mouth lasted long after the treat was devoured. The Boy Housemate is a sweet connoisseur who lives on sugar. He claims you can no longer taste the difference between the M&Ms. It has also become clear that none of the sweets I see are as colourful as they used to be. The packaging is more colourful than ever before, but the sweets themselves have paled. Minus certain E numbers, we are left with a much blander palette of colour in our bag of sweets, and a much more stable spectrum of behaviour from the children who eat them.

I went to a birthday party in a Leisureplex once. The bowling balls were just like giant versions of the gobstoppers they filled us with. Rainbows of sugar and chemicals left within arm's reach in tiny metal bowls after the pizza and cake and before the game of Quasar.

Quasar was a game where we all put on jackets that looked like bulletproof vests with little sensors in the middle, then we were put into this dark, strobe-lit room and the object of the game was to chase each other around with guns while fuelled on sweets until one team had captured the other. When we had tired each other out and our blood-sugar levels had crashed, we would be piled into the back of seatbelt-less cars and driven to the nearest bouncing castle.

Now, children eat dried-fruit pastilles in pastel colours and stay in the same emotional temperature while parents abide by the rules that no home-made treats are acceptable because of food allergies.

Ice-cream hasn't been spared the twenty-first-century revamp either. In the 1990s, we had vanilla, banana, strawberry, chocolate or raspberry ripple, if you were lucky. Now, choosing a flavour is like ordering off a pan-Asian European fusion Michelin-star tasting menu. You can get Belgian Chocolate Roulade Soufflé infused with praline truffles in the shape of Swedish fish all swimming in a heavy dairy notion-filled soup.

As if that weren't excessive, they bring out sorbets and gelato so that those of us who are too virtuous to indulge in the high-fat, high-calorie, *honest* version of dessert can delude ourselves into thinking we are godlike in our abstinence while still getting our RDA of polyols and other fake sugars.

10. Fandom

In second year of secondary school, I spent at least one evening a week in the bedroom of my best friend. We would sit on her bed and tell ghost stories or talk about the people in our class or our teachers. Her mum would bring us food and it was a big treat to be allowed to eat it on the bed while listening to music. I felt so grown up. Even though I must have spent more than a thousand hours in my friend's room, I couldn't tell you what colour her walls were. Why? Because my friend was *obsessed* with Boyzone. Every inch of her walls was enshrined in posters torn out of pop magazines and 'unofficial' annuals. Posters, interviews, T-shirts, CD inserts, ticket stubs, lanyards and anything that would obey the restrictive rules of Blu-tack.

I liked them too, but I never really got into celebrity crushes. I never hung a poster on my wall. I never queued to see anyone and I still can't relate to the impulse of wanting someone's autograph. Why would you want someone to write their name down for you? What is the appeal?

Anyway, my friend was obsessed but she was adorable in her innocent hero-worship. She was a super-fan before celebrities felt the need to protect themselves against super-fans.

I don't know if it's the popularity of shows like *X-Factor*, shows that create megastars who become world famous over a TV season for no other reason than they oversaturate a market. The devastation felt by teenagers across the world when One Direction announced their break-up is not to be dismissed. It's very serious that young people can be so psychologically damaged by the fact that five boys who didn't know each other six years ago have decided not to live on a tour bus together anymore.

That seems innocent when you compare it to the 'cut for Bieber' revolution. That insane phase involved Bieber fans cutting themselves and uploading photos of their bleeding wrists on to Twitter and tagging the young pop star in them in the hope that he might change his party lifestyle.

Where is that trend going to end?

11. Hygiene

I learned to brush my teeth through a song from Barney the Dinosaur. Incidentally, it also taught me about water conservation and to roll my toothpaste from the bottom. Now at night-time, I find myself tired and cold and ready for sleep when I pick up my toothbrush and realise I've forgotten to charge it. I am then faced with the indignity of going over each tooth with the tiniest unmoving head of bristles in the hope that I don't contract gingivitis overnight.

And God forbid two or more toothbrushes need charging. All of my friend's family were home for Christmas and when I arrived to say hello on Christmas Eve I saw six toothbrushes lined up next to the microwave waiting for the charger to become free.

Having a bath on a Sunday night and one again on a Wednesday was enough for me and my peers growing up. Now, it seems that you have to sanitise children each time they pass through a door frame. Certain schools are indistinguishable from hospitals, the wall-mounted sanitising units hanging off the nails where we used to have holy-water fonts.

Our school didn't even get fully involved in the national disinfecting championships of 2001 when foot-and-mouth disease was rampant. We had a massive floor rug doused in disinfectant inside the front door of the school. After the first two hundred feet had mixed their muck with the disinfectant, a puddle of brown water seeped out the side of the floor mat and was so vile that people walked around it, so it might as well not have been there at all.

12. Beds

The humble bed. A place to rest, to lie down and recharge. Now you have 'sleep consultants' in many of the major bedding shops who analyse your sleep position, your marital status and your bank account to see what mattress suits you best. Is it an electronic one that will cost you €3,000 plus the first child conceived therein? A memory foam one that will look like a soup bowl in six months as your hours of rest, coitus and slumber concave it into obscurity? Is it a sprung mattress that your children can bounce on and fall off, opening you up to a family injury lawsuit? The possibilities are endless.

I listen to a lot of podcasts and, recently, they all seem to be sponsored by the same mattress company who make their product sound like it will do so much for you that you need never get out of bed again.

13. Money

I have seen two currency changes in my lifetime – I suspect another is imminent.

The concept of money is difficult to comprehend, even as an adult, because it seems so hard to earn in real life but, when I was growing up, I was given plastic versions of it with most board games, chocolate versions of it at Christmas, edible paper versions of it on summer holidays in seaside towns and piles of it at religious ceremonies I didn't understand.

I still don't know if an actual printed bill represents the digits I see on my online banking. I don't know if there is actual physical cash in a safe somewhere or if it's all just maths.

I did try to figure out why quantitative easing isn't a solution, but I draw the line at Bitcoin.

Bitcoin is the definition of fake money. It is the equivalent of the gold coins I gathered by running Sonic the Hedgehog through a bonus round. I won't even try to understand it anymore because, if I do, I'm likely to try it out and, just like when I downloaded the Paddy Power app during Cheltenham last year, it will only end in tears.

14. Maps

God love my primary-school teachers. They tried as hard as they could to teach us how to read maps. When the sitting down and listening to reason lesson had failed, our proactive primary educators tried a more hands-on method to teach us how to use a physical, printed map.

In fifth class, we went orienteering. Apparently, it's a sport. It didn't feel like a sport. It felt like my teachers had stuck me with two classmates who weren't my friends so we wouldn't be messing, sent us into a forest with a map and a loyalty-card-looking thing, and told us we had two hours to find our way out but we had to use a specific route. They make sure you take the designated route by leaving little stamps tied to trees along the way. When you get to the tree you stamp your loyalty card and know you're on the right track. It's like a low-fat version of Hansel and Gretel.

We got bored. Of course we got bored. It's an excruciating and torturous thing to put eleven-year-olds through. We walked away from the route and sat on a massive rock in the middle of what looked like a stream. I didn't really know the girls, so it was the perfect opportunity to make some new friends. After talking about every other person in our class and finding our common enemies, we noticed that the stream around us had risen massively and, if we had been able to read the map, we would have realised that we were sitting on a rock in a tidal river. We now had no way of getting back to land and the bus was leaving in thirty minutes. We shouted for help but we could tell from what bit of the map we *could* read that we had strayed far from the possibility of being heard.

Just before it got dark, a man walking his dog found us and sent for help. The people who ran the reserve arranged for a tiny boat to cart us back one at a time, to safety. Our class was banned from the Orienteering Championships that year and the one girl who cared never spoke to us again.

I never learned how to read maps and I love the fact that Siri tells me which lane I need to merge with when she gives me directions to places I should know how to get to by now. As I learned in Texas, I am stranded without Siri, but at least I've since become a strong swimmer so I don't feel too bad about my illiteracy in cartography.

15. Household appliances

I got a portable TV for my room from Santa when I was eleven. That thing was no more *portable* than I was. It was about ten kilos and my mother struggled to lift it onto its bracket above my shelves. Things used to say *portable*, but you needed a wheelbarrow to move them. I remember watching kids carrying boomboxes on their shoulders like African women carting enough water for a village back from the well. Today, things are portable, but we're never happy. I overheard a teenager on a bus nagging his mother for an iPad mini because his was too heavy for his schoolbag. I wonder how he would have felt about a Discman.

Hoovers, vacuum cleaners, fans, heaters, hair dryers. Dyson is a company whose sole purpose is to make sure that people who fell into comas ten years ago wake up and do not know what a single household appliance looks like. The ergonomics and futuristic design are mind-blowing.

16. Books

I have a pile of books next to my bed. I call them the Pile of Hope. I always think, when I buy a new book, that I'm also buying the time to read it. This is never the case.

Books have changed unrecognisably since the days of carving symbols into walls. I won't go into the global impact of the printing press because for me a major shift has happened much more recently.

I imagine a massive library, towering mahogany shelves and endless ladders, like something out of Harry Potter, and perched on the shelf, about half way up, is a single shiny Amazon kindle and everything else is bare. Save for a few PhD theses no one will ever read.

I find when I break a €20 note, the small change I get back disappears immediately. I can hold on to a €20 for days at a time but as soon as it is handed back to me in pieces, it evaporates within hours. Coffees, chewing gum, an apple, a car park ticket, a bus ride and it's done. €20 is easy to carry around. It's always really irritating to have coins jingling on your hip like a pocketful of shrapnel. The disappointment when you open a bulging wallet to see layers of coppers lying with a dull smirk under the zip is awful.

Small change is irritating.

Big changes, like spending €49 or a €50 note, are at least noticeable. Someone going from alive to dead isn't sneaky! Small change sneaks up on you. Little alterations in the way life works creep up behind you until you're sitting on a rock surrounded by water and no idea what the future will bring.

16

ALL ABOARD
THE BANDWAGON

'THE BANDWAGON', WHERE MOB MENTALITY
competes with Common Sense in a gruelling but entertaining
fight to the bitter end of logic.

I love a good bandwagon.

Some new crazy thing rolls into town and I am usually the
first to jump on it. I stand at the back of the bandwagon waving
my flag, taking the credit for introducing the world to whatever
it is. My early-adopter badge is worn with the same level of pride
as if I had invented the thing myself.

For a while, I was the girl who brought Harry Potter to Mallow. It's not a title that was given to me in any official way. My mother and I would travel to Cork city on a Saturday and, sometimes, I would buy a book in the massive Waterstones bookshop on Patrick Street. One Saturday, as usual, I bought an unremarkable book, lined up with its spine facing out, just like all of the other books. This was at a time before I or J.K. Rowling knew that within a few short years, children would be lining up at night-time, spines facing out, sheltering from the cold as they queued in the dark of midnight for bookshops to open to sell the next instalment of the Harry Potter saga. I read the first edition of the first one before telling my swimming friends to read it. More than three of them took my word for it and the increase in demand in the small bookshop in my hometown caused the owner to order it in, and thus I take credit for the magic of Harry Potter reaching the millennials of Mallow.

I see bandwagons and crazes as a stockbroker sees shares. If you don't get in early, it's rarely worth it. Part of following trends is that, in order not to feel like the sheep that you are, you have to get in early. You have to mask your blind, manipulated adherence to pop-culture with the smug lie that you were almost part of discovering the trend. That way, by getting involved, you feel like you're disseminating rather than being led. It's like Jesus and his followers. Like many verified Twitter accounts, Jesus had loads of followers but he only had twelve apostles. Those were the early adopters, they weren't just any old followers, they were part of spreading the Good News.

I spread the good news of Beanie Babies, Eircom call cards

and Pokémon cards. I am ashamed to say I also succumbed to the loom-band buzz, but I blame that on the fact that I was trying to quit smoking at the time and I needed something to keep my hands busy. It worked. Although it was well over two years ago now, I'm still finding those tiny elastic bands all over my house. They're like a curse of biblical locusts I can't undo.

I have no such excuse for getting on board with Crocs and I apologise profusely for adding the decorative studs to them in the summer of 2010.

The remnants of each of my phases now have their own corner in my mother's attic. Sitting there, stewing in their rarity and waiting to become relevant again. Sometimes, when the heating comes on or when it's windy and I hear noises in the attic, I wonder if the fourth corner is taken up by the guys from Dexys Midnight Runners – because where did they go? Yes, all the bandwagons in my mother's attic are waiting ... just waiting.

I collected Pokémon cards eventually, but my penchant for catching Pokémon memorabilia started way before then with Pokémon stickers. I spent all of my summers with my nana and grandad in their mobile home in Wexford. I think I loved it so much because the days always played out the same way.

Part of our morning routine was that Nana and I would drive into Gorey to do 'a shop'. After the groceries, we always went to a place called Joanne's Bakery for tea and a cake. Tea never actually featured except in the name of the activity. Nana always got coffee and a cream donut and I always had a coffee slice. Most days we would share. I always got the bigger half. After this, and on our way home, we would stop to buy the papers and, if it was a rainy day, I would be allowed, even encouraged, to get a magazine. There was no such thing as children's TV, and my grandfather had the remote surgically attached to him anyway. On rainy days, my nana needed any support she could get to keep me entertained. On this one day, it came in the form of a sticker book – an orange Pokémon sticker book with 250 blank squares scattered throughout that were to be filled with Bulbasaurs, Charmanders, Pikachus, Jigglypuffs and a Mew, if you were lucky. My nana didn't know it at the time but, in buying that sticker book, our fate for the summer was sealed.

Every day, I would get another pack of ten stickers. Ripping them open, I would shuffle through them to see if I had been gifted with the rare ones I needed. The other kids in the mobile home park got on board and started collecting too. I would rush home with a Charizard knowing that Danny from Baldoyle needed one and he had a Dragonite that I needed. I inhaled my cream bun and ate three-quarters of Nana's, just so we could get home before Raymond from Finglas because he was also looking for a Dragonite and swaps happened on a first-come, first-served basis.

All summer long, I searched for the shiny stickers. They came in slowly until there was only one blank square left in my sticker book. On the kitchen table, piles of 'doubles' and 'triples' lay stacked. The omnipresence of Snorlax and Onix piled next to the salt and pepper shakers. Snorlax's market value had plummeted so much due to product saturation that one of the kids in the park covered the entire side of the see-saw in the playground in stickers of him. Pokémon stickers would blow around the beach town like ash after a volcano, everyone just waiting for Mew. Nana even got involved. She pretended she didn't care, but I saw her eyes light up with hope when she opened a packet of stickers for me. The disappointment etched deep lines into her forehead as she'd exclaim, defeated, 'Only another load of aul Digletts. Those Digletts are like aul wasps around the place.'

I got Mew in a packet of stickers I bought at a petrol station on the N11 outside Greystones. My 99 ice-cream dripped down my grandfather's hand as I instructed him to hold it and not lick it while I placed my last sticker into the book. I think Nana was disappointed I didn't wait for her to put it in. Our summer was complete and so was our sticker book. A twenty-page book that must have had at least €1,000 invested in it. ''Twas worth it, mind you. That was a great summer,' she says now.

Pokémon threatened to take another summer of mine hostage in 2016. In August of that year, I couldn't walk down a street in Dublin or New York – where I was working – without seeing terrifying droves of people glued to their phones. I caught the words 'Pokémon Go' in the seconds of conversation I snatched as people walked by me or as they sat in cafés. The game plunged into my reality and into the phones of millions.

Pokémon Go was a miracle in certain respects. I saw people I knew out and about for the first time since they invented the PlayStation. Gamers who had been decomposing in dark rooms in front of flat-screen TVs and pizza boxes were suddenly moving at a brisk pace to catch the Chansey on the roof of a passing bus.

Before I fully understood what Pokémon Go was, my friend from the US arrived in Dublin to stay with me for a week. She isn't American, she was born and raised within walking distance of a DART line, so I found it really confusing when she started requesting that we go and visit all of these Dublin landmarks for our 'quality-time' activities.

We had been to the Guinness Storehouse, Áras an Uachtaráin and Dublin Zoo before I realised what was happening. As we wiggled our way through a group of Japanese tourists near the statue of Molly Malone, I had to stop and ask her what the hell she was playing at. She explained that she had been bitten hard by the Pokémon Go craze. She was comfortably seated and fully strapped into the bandwagon. She was beyond saving. She had even invested in a pricey portable phone charger to mitigate the outrageous battery drainage that was a complaint with the game. She said that Pokémon spawned best in tourist locations and they were geo-tagged so there were ones you could catch in Ireland that you could never find in New York. She explained the reason we had been running through Irish landmarks was because the Pokémon disappeared within fifteen minutes so she was frantically trying to get as much as she could out of each neighbourhood.

We sat in my local café, which happened to be a Poké Stop. I know this because as soon as the café owner realised that they had been granted Poké Stop status from across the world by the creators of the game, he started to advertise it on a chalkboard outside the door. I asked the owner and he said they definitely saw a peak in sales because of it.

As my friend held her phone in the air trying to catch one of the invisible animals flying around the café, I scrolled through the news. A girl in California had been stabbed while playing Pokémon Go in a park. Her injuries weren't life-threatening, but when her friend had tried to come to her rescue she was beaten in the neck with a pipe and mugged.

In Florida, a sixteen-year-old and a nineteen-year-old were playing the game in their car. They pulled up outside a house and ran onto a lawn to catch one of the digital critters when the owner of the house came out and shot at them. In New York, a man crashed into a tree while playing and two people in San Diego fell off a cliff.

I wonder what sort of rare Pokémon Nana and I would have found in Joanne's Bakery in Gorey. What untimely demise would we have come to if we had got into Pokémon Go the way we got into Pokémon stickers?

My cousin and I spent a few years in a blur of dazed and frenzied consumerism. As young adults, we teetered on the brink of insanity, dragging our parents and their bank accounts to the brink with us. Together, we abandoned all sense of decency and proportion as we scavenged toy shop bins for plush toys with their labels intact. The Ty Beanie Baby craze was possibly one of the best marketing campaigns in history.

Beanie Babies were a phenomenon before they became a bandwagon. It's hard, from the outside, to distinguish when that shift happens, and from the inside it's nigh on impossible.

Ty Warner, now known as Ty Inc, were extremely clever in their marketing. They played into my sense of future insecurity and my desperate need to be liked and to fit in. They intentionally created a limited stock of cute toys with human attributes, like names and a birthday, and they were very clear on the rules. They said in no uncertain terms, *this* beanie baby will be on sale for six months and, after that, it will be discontinued. Unlike most parents that you see on *Supernanny*, the company Ty followed through with their threat and didn't give in to the shouts and screams of the childish public for more. It was like a primitive form of viral marketing. It was completely dependent on the human condition of liking things that other people don't know about yet. Just like introducing a town to Harry Potter or teaching 'native savages' how to use cutlery, having a rare beanie baby made you feel like you had some coolness capital.

I watched as my relatives hit rock bottom, begging friends of friends who were going to America to bring back wholesale packets of 'tag protectors'. In America, you see, they sold the little plastic hearts that protected the tags hanging off the Beanie Babies' ears. Without their tags attached, Beanie Babies were utterly worthless. Without the little heart that contains their name and a four-line poem about them, the Beanie Baby undergoes the same transformation into obscurity as if you took the title of 'Queen' from Elizabeth herself.

In Ireland, the tag protectors were €4 each but you could get ten for $10 in America. Young, bored entrepreneurs were taking transatlantic flights to wherever was cheapest and stocking up to come home and make their millions from us island-bound buffoons.

In the brightness of Garcia the tie-dyed bear or Chops the Lamb and Chocolate the Moose, we became blind to the actual value of the items we were buying. It was one of the first times I saw a product ostensibly marketed at pocket-money-wielding kids being as attractive to middle-aged hobbyists.

We swapped reason and sense for the jittery, adrenaline-filled fervour of amassing disproportionate quantities of stuffed animals. That was part of the charm, for me anyway. These toys weren't just stuffed with your average cotton substitute stuffing. They were heavy and substantial with the PVC pellets that they were packed with. The weight of them made them great for lobbing ... onto a shelf ... and never moving off it. Ever. They were designed to just sit there and gather dust.

When the company Ty Warner brought out a small number of Black Bears called The End, the insanity reached new heights. We didn't know if it was the end of all Beanie Babies or if it was just the limited millennium-edition bear. The most crazed of fans shelled out thousands for The End and if we hadn't found one in a discount bin in a gift shop in the Crescent Shopping Centre in Limerick, The End would have been just that for us. My family rode the Beanie Baby bandwagon to near bankruptcy.

But the family lost a little bit of respect for Ty Warner when they tried to capitalise on Princess Diana's death in 1997 with an extremely rare and limited edition bear. We all agreed it was uncouth to turn a profit from the death of a princess and we were told never to buy the bear in a small protest against their opportunism. It may have been a ruse to stop us from using all the dial-up internet minutes searching online for the commemorative relic.

I had terrible asthma as a child. Our entire house was carpeted in Laura Ashley high-pile and so it was with great upset that my mother, having been instructed by my GP, got rid of the carpet in my room and replaced it with wooden tongue-and-groove slats. It took a few weeks for her to get used to it. I could hear the exhale and the disappointment in her breathing as she mourned the dense saxony pile that once was. Keeping my lungs clear was one thing, but keeping her home looking like something out of a Martha Stewart magazine was another.

I can't fully blame my mother or the Beanie Babies or the weak bronchioles in my chest for the Great Asthma Attack of 2002. I had grown tired of the incessant chase for more Beanie Babies. The ones I owned had lost their appeal but they sat on my shelf – a heavy, stationary representation of my capitalist, consumerist guilt. They gathered so much dust because I never used them or had any reason to move them, because they *did* nothing. They had no use other than to sit there, gathering around them my dead skin cells and other floating bacteria, storing it up in an arsenal to throw back at me one day when I unsettled them.

I had heard that one of my Beanie Babies might be worth something. It was a first edition brown monkey called Nana, which was re-released later as Bongo. Apparently, Nana was very valuable, and I knew I had one because the name was the only reason it had been bought for me. Climbing up to my shelf to find Nana with the intention of selling it for a high price, the gods of justice and comeuppance struck me down. As I moved the plush toys and they all fell onto the bed, layers of dust rose in the daylight into my lungs and set off an asthma attack.

I thought it was karma for being willing to sell something called Nana.

The Beanie Babies were put in the attic in the hope that they would age like a good wine and pay for my college fees. They're still there. A bit like real pensions, what we were told was a legitimate investment opportunity became devalued and worthless almost overnight. The astronomically inflated value of years of hunting and gathering had amounted to nothing.

I love bandwagons because they make me feel included. There is a unison about them, and a feeling of solidarity in going through a trend with your peers. There is a false sense that everyone in the world is playing by the same rules and that you are all singing from the same hymn sheet. It's comforting to think that you are part of a community who share the same views, likes and dislikes as you. There's a safety in the mob mentality of it.

Bandwagons are not limited to consumerism. In the run-up to the 2016 US presidential election, the news coverage and echo chambers of social media constructed a bandwagon of Trojan Horse proportions. You weren't a socially conscious person unless you had at least one tweet or meme making fun of Donald Trump. The mob mentality around hating Trump made me believe we were all on the same bandwagon and his winning would be impossible and ludicrous.

And then in November 2016, Donald Trump went from being this novelty meme-machine nominee to being the US President Elect.

I arrived in Dallas, Texas, the day after Donald Trump was elected. I suspected that everyone would be as shocked as I was at the news. I anticipated seeing the memes I had seen online printed and blown-up into billboard proportions in reaction to the outrage that had become so supersized that it could not be contained within digital confines.

What I was confronted with was far different. There was no such outrage, there was no bandwagon for me to board. I was, for the first time in a long time, in the minority.

I stood outside the World Rodeo Championships in Dallas, trying to get some air. Inside, the arena heaved with excited moustaches hidden under cowboy hats. There was only one iconic red 'Make America Great Again' hat to be seen in the venue that housed 45,000 people.

I met a lady named Martha in the lift of my hotel. She gave me the biggest hello I had received in years. One of those 'hellos' that makes you feel instantly guilty, as though you should not just know the person already, but should also know their birthday. I saw her again outside the arena. We queued up together to exchange our dollars for 'Man Bucks', the currency accepted at the Rodeo Championships.

As we queued up, I noticed there were cacti, like alien shapes backlit by the glow from the neon lights of the city, sprawling around us. A stallion passed between the cacti and the glow, making its way inside to compete. Martha told me the horse belonged to Turtle Powell, and he was a sure bet to win tonight's 'calf-wrestling' event. She followed my gaze and enlightened me further.

'That cactus there is agave.'

I've only ever seen the word written down. She pronounced it 'ah-gah-vay', like 'ah-gah-vay Maria'.

Agave is the healthy replacement for sugar that has finally made its way to Ireland and has taken over your porridge and protein balls in recent months. The plants looked beautiful and exotic. They were not the size of the novelty cactus I'd bought as a houseplant in Woodies DIY because the salesman told me they were impossible to kill and thrived on neglect.

It was loud at the rodeo. People were dressed as cowboys but they weren't in costume or being ironic. People were cheering and hugging, every single person who passed smiled at me as I queued for refreshments. There was a wall of soft drinks, unrefrigerated, behind the counter. The sugar sediment in them had sunk to the bottom of the bottles, gathering, making it look like a wall of expired egg timers.

If the bottles of soda represented America, and the sugary-sweet sediment was the happiness at the presidential election result, then Texas at that time was the bottom of the American fizzy drink. All of the happiness, joy and hope seemed to have drained from above, pooled there and settled.

It was baffling, but the hope in Texas at that time was palpable and contagious. It was an audacious, gun-carrying kind of hope for the future, and for change by the people who had merely tolerated Obama. There was a real sense of 'y'all had your turn at hope – now it's ours'. I didn't experience any malice in it but I was aware that cacti look very beautiful but on inspection they have spikes and they hurt if you get close. The spikes thrive on neglect.

The smiles and snippets I caught at the gas station or at the rodeo were like the soundbites I heard on the streets of Dublin in May 2015, the day after Ireland voted yes to marriage equality. The public morale seemed high in Texas.

At the opening of the rodeo, the MC prayed 'to the Lord Jesus Christ to keep our cowboys safe for this event'.

It was around Veterans Day too, so two bearded men in dirty denim hoisted an octogenarian out of his seat while the TV cameras captured it all on a forty-foot screen. The man had fought at Iwo Jima. The crowd went wild. The MC then introduced a young, fresh-faced cadet who was heading away to fight 'for this great land'. The two screens created an illusion where the octogenarian was facing the cadet. It was poignant and intense and then the beat dropped and Iggy Azalea kicked in, I suspect, to rile up the horses and bulls.

I kept quiet about my views and fears of Trump in Texas. I was in the minority, so I didn't really feel safe to start a discussion. For the first time, the thought occurred to me that this is what had happened to this silent majority during Obama's reign. It became unacceptable and impossible to criticise liberalism from the right in any legitimate way, so they stayed quiet. As my colleague from New York, who was travelling with me, asked on seeing the celebrations around us, 'Is what I am feeling now how the racists felt when Obama was elected?' He was withered from the result.

But it hadn't changed their minds, just as being silent about my views at the rodeo hadn't changed my mind. All of their unspoken views had just sunk to the bottom, waiting, waiting for someone like Trump to come and shake them up and mobilise the sediment.

The Republicans have thrived on neglect.

There's a definite agave sweetness down there in Texas. It's not quite the sweetness we're used to, it's not the sugary comfort we grew up with but, in these bitter times, will agave do? Is some hope somewhere, held by a few, better than none?

Oh, and Turtle Powell, the 'sure bet' that Martha told me about?

He didn't win.

He came second.

Maybe next time.

I really thought that Donald Trump was a bandwagon, but it wasn't the first political campaign that saw millions of people jumping aboard to get involved in the cause. In 2012, in what genuinely seemed like a matter of hours, the whole world seemed to suddenly become aware that Uganda existed. This was long after films like *Hotel Rwanda*, *Tears of the Sun* and *Blood Diamond* had highlighted the turbulent political landscape in war-torn Africa. In one day, a social activist group called Innocent Children uploaded a video that went viral in an instant. The biggest social-justice bandwagon had been born and people were scrambling in their millions to get on board.

The video played into the popular phenomenon of armchair activists or slacktivists. You didn't have to do anything except share the video or maybe buy a bracelet for $19 to feel like you were playing your part in trying to track down and catch Joseph Kony. Kony 2012 became a hashtag that trended worldwide for weeks. The well-crafted video shared online confronted the myopic world view of the adolescents sharing it and made us all feel like we could actually do something to help.

In ways it worked. It *did* put Uganda on the map as a dangerous place where people's human rights were being violated, but it also highlighted the difference between bandwagons and raising awareness.

They didn't find Joseph Kony, which isn't surprising because unless he was going to check-in online somewhere, no one was going to catch him. Behind a laptop screen, the illusion of agency is just that. An illusion. We were confronted with a horrible reality that kids were being kidnapped and tortured, but to make sure we didn't feel too discomfited by it, we could alleviate the guilt of our incapacity and were given the chance to simply share the video and get on with our day, feeling like virtuous warriors of social injustice. I'm as guilty as anyone. I think I even put a KONY2012 twibbon on my Facebook profile. The sad part is, I can't even remember.

We got back to New York after our Texas trip and, sitting in a café in Williamsburg, eating kale chips that had been served to me in a deconstructed shoe box and drinking ethically sourced cold-brew coffee from a mason jar, I questioned when a bandwagon stops being a bandwagon and becomes some sort of normal.

Have hipsters and their studiously thought-out socks been

around too long to legitimately be a bandwagon? To give them their due, they have really held their own in the face of blatant public hatred and sustained ridicule.

I never condone the mass ridicule of a minority group, but I find hipsters particularly hard to defend, even though I know a few of them personally. Having gentrified our entire neighbourhood with their Victorian beards and collarless shirts, they are now hell bent on driving up the price of Brussels sprouts at our local farmers' market. Brussels sprouts have been there all along, just doing their thing, polarising families over Christmas dinner but then, just like a heat-seeking missile, hipsters set their sights on them and in no time they have become the food of the elite.

It is possible that they have protected themselves from being labelled a bandwagon because, to this day, I have never heard someone self-identify as a hipster. It's as if they are too cool to call themselves cool. Even when they stand before you sporting a Victorian beard and headphones plugged into a turntable playing a record of a band no one will hear of for another decade, a true hipster will outright refuse to identify as such. They will claim their hirsute lumber-sexual look is just thrown together and will stomp off offended towards the closest bowl of quinoa.

A friend of mine is now on a massive quinoa buzz. This has followed the goji berry buzz, the avocado buzz and just raw things in general. Apart from the strain this is putting on her bank account – having to restock her entire kitchen every time a new issue of American *Vogue* hits the shelves – it's also putting a strain on our relationship. The look of disgust that comes over her when I haven't heard of the superfood du jour or when I reach for a carbohydrate is exhausting.

The bandwagon of what we should be eating changes so quickly it's like the specials menu in a fish restaurant. Never has a bandwagon been so difficult to keep up with. The idea that you will die alone from a degenerative illness if you don't infuse your water with cucumber and mint is just not something I can get on board with. Can I not just fill my empty Volvic bottle from my tap, no?

I get really unnerved when the bandwagon rolls out of town. I imagine myself running down the street after the wagon, all my call cards, Beanie Babies and Pokémon cards falling out of the bundle in my arms and leaving a trail of accumulated detritus in my wake. I shout for the bandwagon to stay in town and not to leave – after all, what am I meant to do with €1,200 worth of cuddly toys?

Our Pokémon house of cards came crashing around us, Pikachus tumbling to the floor like their market value and we, the collectors, reassured ourselves with the notion that they'll be worth something one day. We always stand up again, brush ourselves off and wait at the side of the road for the next thing to come along and pick us up.

17
GENDERALISATIONS

MY PRIMARY SCHOOL WAS A HEALTHY-EATING school. There was an outright ban on sugary treats and chocolate. Keep in mind that this was a time before people weaponised vegetables, the days when Sunny-D and Ribena were seen as healthy alternatives. In these health-conscious times, it seems that printing 'HIGH PROTEIN' or 'LOW SUGAR' will delude people into thinking the product is healthy but, in my primary-school days, it was 'LOW FAT' that had crisps flying off the shelves. That was before we met our first avocado or almond in Ireland and learned that there are such things as 'good' fats.

Tayto brought out a range of on-trend crisps just at the peak of the low-fat bell curve. In order to alleviate any doubt that they were healthy, the packaging was slightly lighter in colour and was emblazoned with the title of the crisps in a wavy font, presumably to reinforce the idea that these were less heavy and threatening than their common-or-garden cheese-and-onion brethren. The crisps were so unthreatening to your waistline that they were given initials as their name. Their impact on your daily calorie intake was as minimal as three letters, LFC – Low Fat Crisps.

We had seen our mothers pick them up in stores as the *healthy* option. It stood to reason in our young minds that they would be allowed in our packed lunches – they were, after all, *healthy*.

But, when the vice-principal of our school confiscated thirteen bags of LFCs from the fifth- and sixth-class students over one lunch period, we set about planning a coup. It was Shauna who was the most outraged at losing her contraband and organised a meeting in the fifth-class toilets. As we gathered around the hand dryer in the freezing, green-tiled bathroom, I was nominated by everyone to be the voice of reason. I was pushed to the top of the group to deliver the opening salvos to the vice-principal. I prepared and rehearsed a measured argument with quotations from the back of an empty bag of LFCs we found in the bottom of Josephine's schoolbag. I was democratically chosen to carry the message of my peers to the policy-makers of St Mary's Convent Primary School. There were sixty girls on board with the decision even though only thirteen of them were directly involved, but we all refused to take part in our maths class in solidarity with the Hungry Ones. We won the argument and the girls got their crisps back and I was hailed a hero for the rest of the week.

When I took it upon myself to convince the same vice-principal that it was unconstitutional to make us go outside for PE in winter, I did not rank so highly in the polls of popular opinion in my class. When our teacher stopped bringing us outside to play rounders, the sporty girls stopped talking to me and held it against me for an entire season.

In a way, I'm lucky that I learned this lesson at such a tender age. I do not speak for groups larger than me, myself and I, unless I am democratically elected to do so. I do not speak for my entire gender nor do I speak for my entire generation. However, in being given a loudspeaker by doing the work that I do, my word is often taken as *the* word on a subject, my opinions are taken as some yardstick, a measure against which all women/millennials can be measured. This is never my intention. Every person is the centre of their own world and has a set of influences and histories that changes how they experience the world.

I just want to shine a light on the things that I see, the things that I read and think about, and speak about the world I experience from where I am at. If I touch on generational or gender issues, then that is great, but I am never trying to propose that my opinion is shared by anyone other than just me. I know girls I went to school with who live in rural Ireland. They pay mortgages on four-bedroom detached properties with planning permission to extend. They pay voluntary contributions to pensions every week and are on their third planned child.

How could I possibly be their voice? I can't even commit to an eighteen-month phone contract.

I met a sensational girl at an awards ceremony last year. Razan Ibraheem is a Syrian journalist who came to Ireland to study and, when war broke out, found that she couldn't return home. She speaks about watching her city, her country and her people being destroyed and crumbling under the weight of the war ravaging the Middle East. She is also a millennial. She is also a woman. How could I possibly call myself her voice?

This chapter is the hardest one to write in a way because it seems that, these days, as a young woman, I am obliged to have certain views or gripes or desires to advocate for specific causes. My opinion on major national issues shouldn't be as weighted as it sometimes is. These are not my thoughts on feminism as a movement or as a cause of social justice, it is simply my experience of being a woman in the world. For no other reason than that is what I am.

I would be defacing an entire generation and an entire gender by claiming my experience is the general one. As they say on Twitter: *All opinions are my own and RTs do not equal endorsements*.

Feminism is a flashpoint. Sometimes, it feels to me like a clique that I am not allowed to be part of unless I wear a certain type of jumper or retweet a certain opinion. I sometimes feel excluded from it because, unless you are a particularly specific *type* of woman with a highly curated set of views and principles, you are not allowed to call yourself a feminist.

I am speaking, as I said, from my own experience, which I now realise is one of remarkable privilege. I had never considered myself in terms of my gender until I saw it continually tagged onto descriptions of me when *Can't Cope, Won't Cope* aired. The mass media thought it absolutely vital that people knew I was not just a writer but I was also not a male writer.

My mother loves to host dinner parties with her friends. She really comes into her own in summer when the long evenings afford her the time to have people round for barbecues. Every May, she has the same realisation. Without learning from her annual mistake from all previous years, one mild evening in early summer, my mother will realise that she has left the barbecue uncovered for the entire winter. As she holds rusty tongs and weather-beaten grates up at me through the window, we start the same debate. Will she get another year out of the barbecue? Every three or four years, the answer is no. One summer, we had done this dance and ended up in our local garden centre. When we chose the barbecue that would see us through the next few years, weather dependent, the guy at the counter served us and winked at me as he put the massive box onto one of those flat trolleys. 'Will you help your dad to put this together later?' he asked. I looked at him confused, looked to my mother, back to him then laughed with my mother as if to say, *This guy, huh?*

There was never a time in my life where the absence of a man was a presence in our house. As I saw it, some people had brothers and some people didn't; some had dads and others didn't. My mother never seemed to require male assistance for anything. She installed televisions, carved turkeys, paid bills and erected Christmas trees. She changed plugs with the same precision she changed lightbulbs and tyres, and it was all extremely unremarkable. If something needed doing, Mam did it, whether it was putting a stitch in a torn garment or putting up a roller blind. Seeing her operate at this level, and also watching my nana running her own business, meant that I didn't have eye-witness examples of gender inequality as a child. I grew up blind to gender-specific roles and the idea of gender as a barrier to progress.

In fact, I have never experienced gender bias in any way that I can name. The one time I was ever wolf-whistled at in the street, I was thrilled because it felt like a watershed moment in trying to lose weight.

The women who surrounded me in my formative years were far from bit-players. They were institutions. In my fourteen years of primary and secondary education, I was taught by four men in total. One was a substitute teacher we had for a week in fifth class, and he was the only male educator I interacted with until I was thirteen. In secondary school, I was taught Geography, Science and Economics by men.

My nana is the knot that binds all of the strands of our family together. She ran her own pharmacy business while also managing the accounts for my grandfather's construction company and raising five children on home-cooked meals. When I came along and it looked like I would be raised in Germany, before my parents divorced, my grandmother took the mornings off work to travel to the Goethe Institute in Fitzwilliam Square to learn German so she could communicate with me.

Comparatively, my impressions of men in my early years were fairly uninspiring.

When American teenagers from transatlantic TV shows would preach to me about 'dating' or 'have a crush' on Zack Morris or whoever it was, I could never relate to the impulse. Boys were *grand*, like.

As I reached my teenage years, I started to learn some of the value men could bring to a situation. They were handy to have on your sports team because they were fast and didn't care about making enemies by winning. They were better to hang out with if you wanted to climb trees or play conkers or get messy by playing hide and seek. They were a bit stupider but that made everything less complicated. When Danny insulted me on the green one day and didn't pick up that I was sulking, I learned after two hours that he hadn't meant it as an insult and so wouldn't ever pick up on my subtle signals of upset so I might as well drop it.

When my hormones got shuffled around and resettled, I very clearly understood the reason men were put on the earth. All of the attention I hadn't paid to men in my early years had been saved inside me, stored up, to be unleashed on innocent, unknowing men for years to come.

In my teenage years, I was 'one of the lads'. Aside from the fact that my carapace of obesity disqualified me from being sexually attractive to teenage boys, I simply found their company less complicated and dramatic. Spending all of my school hours surrounded by girls sometimes gave me the feeling, had the film existed then, that we were in a version of *The Hunger*

Games where the object was to undermine each other to the death. With my male friends, it was refreshingly, if not mind-numbingly, simple.

I have never apologised to a male colleague.

I have never needed to apologise to a male colleague, nor has one ever apologised to me or needed to. More and more, I find that when I meet female colleagues, we just apologise *at* each other, almost as a sustained greeting.

It's time for us to not be afraid to do business in a direct way. It's time we learned that we have nothing to apologise for and being direct, officious and business-like does not make us any less 'good' or 'worthy' or 'likeable'.

Outside of my mother and grandmother, I have mentioned before how influential *Sabrina the Teenage Witch* was to me. The whole show was radical in its 1990s feminism but in one episode Sabrina (because of her cat's interference with one of her spells), and everyone else ends up sent back in time to the 1960s and she is shocked at the grossly different way women are treated. Her best friend is no longer editor of the school paper, or wears jeans to school because 'I'm a girl'. And Sabrina can't apply to the university she has her eye on because they don't admit women.

She eventually manages to undo the disaster and everyone is hurtled back to the present with some life lessons and appreciation for where they are at. With a new respect for the suffragettes, Sabrina makes a promise to continue the fight for women's rights. And she does … until the credits roll anyway.

A quote from her teacher Mrs Quick sort of sums up the

whole lesson of the episode – though at the time I absorbed it without any of its subtext or morality – 'Men rule the world, and they do it by oppressing women, forcing us into stereotypical roles and shoes that create permanent foot problems ... remember, a woman without a man is like a fish without a bicycle.'

Maybe I haven't had my Sabrina moment yet.

I believe that I would fight to the death if I saw a woman being treated differently for no reason other than her gender, but I haven't seen that. I have seen gender bias weaponised and used as an excuse for mediocrity. I have also seen brilliant women be less successful than equally talented men. Maybe the lack of opportunity she has been given is down to gender? I don't know. Maybe I am too afraid to believe that gender bias exists because I don't want to see myself as some sort of victim.

I do remember feeling like aspects of my femininity should be kept secret. Our whole class would giggle uncomfortably if the word *sex* was mentioned in Science, even if our teacher was using the *gender* meaning of the word. There was a special shame held for people who said the word *orgasm* instead of *organism* when reading aloud in class. Those students were never the same again.

Sex was something we learned about as purely practical. It was something you did when you wanted to have a baby, and only then. This has definitely screwed with my mind and the minds of my Catholic-raised girl friends. It has probably damaged our sex lives irreversibly. It wasn't men who were telling us to roll down our skirts. It wasn't men who told us that it was indecent for girls to smoke or use curse words. It certainly wasn't men who shunned Martina O'Keeffe when she got pregnant in fifth year. It was women. It was teachers and nuns and other people's mothers. Mothers who mother by discipline, Calpol and respecting your elders.

I suspect that in reaction to not wanting to appear like we have been given an 'easy ride', I am more prone to demanding that women prove their worth. I don't like the idea of gender quotas because it makes my achievements feel less valid. I often feel like I am on some kind of scheme when people talk about me in terms of a percentage in a statistic that is the basis for an argument about getting more money for 'women's' projects. I want my work to stand out for its own sake and not the fact that it's written by a woman.

Adding my gender to a description of me supposes that I should not be as talented as I am *because* I am female. Men and women alike absorb that expectation and operate under its influence. That is the reason I am harder on women.

Katrina Lynch found out two months before our Leaving Cert that she was dyslexic. She was one of two girls in our year who were offered extra time to sit each of the state exam papers in their own private room with access to a person to read the paper to them to make it easier. Katrina didn't take them up on the offer. Margaret did. Margaret Flynn had been given the same diagnosis when we were in third class. Now, seeing as how you can't *contract* dyslexia, it's safe to say that Katrina Lynch was always dyslexic but because she didn't have the diagnosis to use as an excuse for not doing homework or learning essays, she was slightly more competent but miles more confident when the exams came around. Margaret had always been told she would find reading and writing hard and was given aid at every opportunity and, through no fault of her own, had come to see herself as lacking in ability in school.

I don't like to think of myself as needing extra support to get through my life or career because of the body I was born with. I don't appreciate when women use their gender as an excuse for their lack of career success or personal achievement. Maybe that is completely unacceptable for me to say. Maybe I am lacking tremendously in empathic imagination and have no ability to see outside of my own experience. If I had proof that a man was equally skilled and qualified as me and was getting ahead just because he had a penis and more testosterone, I would be fucking furious and would kick up such a shit storm that it wouldn't be worth it for any man to get in my way. I just don't have that proof.

When *Can't Cope, Won't Cope* aired in 2016, there were several middle-aged men who, without wanting to seem critical or cynical, genuinely couldn't understand the mass appeal and attention that the show garnered. I feel that it is inelegant to rebut criticisms of my work but, also, I didn't blame these guys for not understanding it.

Middle-aged, heterosexual, white men have spent their entire lives having things made *for them*. They have been the target audience of popular consumerism since consumerism became a thing. Cinema has been constructed to appeal to them. Crash-test dummies were only male in form until 2003, which meant a much higher female mortality rate. Hand tools are designed for male hands. Public seating is designed to be comfortable for a specific leg length – the leg length of the average man. Hand rails on trains and buses are often too high for women to reach. Our world and all of its tributaries have been designed with the male user/viewer/consumer in mind – from the height of an average step on a staircase to food portion size. And, if you grow up with the whole world designed to make your experience of it comfortable and safe for you, then it must be alarming and unsettling to be confronted with half an hour of television that is simply not made for you. It might be the first thing you come across that has not considered your opinion of it, at all.

I wouldn't have gone as far as Nestlé did when they designed the wrapper for Yorkie bars though. The chocolate bar conveying the message 'It's not for girls' made it as simple as it could so men would know this was just for them. I sympathise with men who met their first female Yorkie equivalent in the shape of my TV show. It's only twenty-seven minutes a week though. There are 10,053 minutes left in every week to make them feel secure again.

A white-hot anger does come over me when I am faced with evidence of injustice, particularly violence against women in other countries. It's a frustrated choking sort of anger in my throat, where I feel powerless to do anything because how can you negotiate with men who outright believe that they have a higher status than women and that means they can treat them however they want?

As a woman, I sometimes walk around in a heightened consciousness. You know when you're walking home in the dark and you're so hyper alert that it's like your whole body becomes an eye? Speaking to the Boy Housemate, it seems that he has experienced this phenomenon of being supersensitive and vigilantly present only when he's walking through empty streets at night having recently watched a horror film.

Since I lost weight, I don't look as strong as I am. Perhaps I should rephrase that as – when I was fat, I looked a lot stronger than I was. Men are less inclined to try to overpower someone who is bigger than them. At my class in Martial Arts Inc., we have done several self-defence tutorials because the reality is that by becoming a smaller target, I increased the likelihood of being targeted.

I sometimes feel that anxiety has taken up residence in my chest so that I have to remind myself to breathe. I am aware that I am physically weaker than most men. When it's dark outside and I am walking home, even if it's only 5 p.m. in winter, my mind goes into overdrive. I think, *What can I hear? What am I near? Who is looking at me? What are they thinking? How do I appear? Am I standing as tall as I can and taking up as much physical space as possible? If someone attacked me right now is there something I could grab? Is there someone within earshot? What would I shout?* I walk with my hand clasped around my iPhone so I can call someone if something goes down. I know I'd never use it for fear of seeming hysterical. I wouldn't call someone unless I was 100 per cent sure something sinister was happening, and by then it would be too late. Still, I grab my phone. It's better to be safe than to be sorry. But it's better to be unobtrusive than safe.

I am going to contradict myself here – and I reserve the right to do so because this is a really complex issue and I don't even really know how I feel about it all – I do *sometimes* feel burdened by being a woman. It's a burden I'm not quite ready to share though.

The burden carried by women worldwide to make sure they don't get pregnant is one that is starting to shift. I have recently read about a new male contraceptive gel that blocks the sperm before they're able to make it out of the man. That's all well and good, and it is high time that there is an alternative to women taking hormones on a daily basis. The contraceptive pill is fine for some, but I know some of my friends feel like someone has taken a meat tenderiser to their endocrine system when they take it – their moods swing like a piñata and every interaction feels like someone is taking a swing at them with a baseball bat. However, I am not sure that I trust men with the almighty power of contraception. Giving the power of contraception back to men and ceding the control that women fought so hard to achieve seems like a step in the wrong direction. Imagine if they got rid of all female contraceptives and just left us with this male gel and the hope we won't conceive? We would be livid. In Ireland, too many men already make decisions for women they will never meet. I like the *idea* that men are willing to share the burden of birth control with us, but I also like the *idea* that if I am not ready to grow a baby inside me right now, that's fully within my control.

The role of women in society is changing. Some are fighting to cast off the concept of having a 'role' at all. Some want to dispense with an archaic patriarchal template of what they should be. Some are desperately clinging on to the old ways because the new, unknown form of femininity is crippling. Am I meant to let you pay for my meal or am I meant to fight to pay for it myself? Am I allowed to enjoy wearing make-up or should I feel my eyelids closing with the heavy weight of patriarchal eye-shadow expectations of beauty? Should I have kids or not? If I have them, can I go back to work and employ someone to bottle-feed them or will I be arrested? There are so many moving parts to being a woman today that it makes my ovaries tremble.

I like to know where I stand. When you go to get your passport renewed, you have to take a ticket with a number on it and wait for it to be called. It's clear, civilised and reassuring in its simplicity. Sometimes, it's comforting to be told where your place is. It's not comforting if your place is always at the bottom, in the corner, seen and not heard, and I know that it is progressive that we are working towards gender parity.

I might find it comforting to be told my place in line at the passport office, but that's only because someone fought for me to be allowed to have a passport in the first place.

18

EMBRACE CHANGE

ALL THESE CHANGES THAT I CAN'T COPE WITH KEEP coming at me and yet there are things that seriously need to change and they still haven't. Here are a few from my list of things that need to change.

1. Computer antivirus software. They've basically cured smallpox, measles and polio to name a few – how come computer viruses are still a thing?

2. The theme tune to *Two and a Half Men*.

3. The way earphones get tangled up even when you leave them sitting on a flat surface. You come back and they've tied themselves into a CIA-worthy ball of tanglement.

4. CCTV footage. I can take a standard of photo on my iPhone that classes as award-winning and yet anytime I watch *Crime Call*, they're asking me to identify a man who looks like something out of an 8-bit video game.

5. Clarity of announcements in stations and on public transport. If there is a PA system, then it's obviously necessary that the public hear the message but it all sounds like a call to prayer in a language I don't speak.

6. Ink cartridges. Why can I not print in black ink when my cyan colour is empty? I'M NOT TRYING TO USE CYAN.

7. iMessage. How have Apple not included an update that would let me have a sarcasm font when I am texting? Or at least bold *and* italic?

8. Let's start giving people control of their own bodies maybe?

9. Have a global common plug and socket combo.

10. Appliances. Can we change it so that my oven knows when my porridge scones are cooked because I have no way of telling from the outside? And can the tumble dryer detect when my clothes are dry and not go on to shrink them into obscurity?

11. Taxi apps. Inventing a button on a taxi app where you can select 'please don't talk to me' for the introverts in the world.

12. The fact that you have to be at the airport two hours before a fifty-five-minute flight.

13. The fact that driving from Dublin to Cork takes the same amount of time as getting the train.

14. Stupid dress codes. I really do believe that you should dress for the job that you have and that it is respectful to suit up on certain occasions, but the idea that I can't eat lunch with my friends because I'm wearing runners is a bit much.

15. Being able to walk into a store in some places, when you're seething with rage, and allowed to buy a gun.

16. Guitars that catch the plectrums before they fall inside.

17. Door handles that catch in your belt loop.

18. Stickers that don't peel off in one go and leave that awful glue residue on stuff.

19. Touchscreen keypad tones being switched on as a default.

19

BUT WHY DOES IT RHYME?

When I was a kid, I used to get scared,
like if I had an exam and had nothing prepared
or even small things like being alone in the dark
or the fear when I swam of being eaten by sharks.
Since I can remember, I've had this fear,
but one day I managed to make it disappear.
During this panic, my heart would start racing,
pounding in my chest, so I started by placing

my little shaky hand over my heart,
I could feel each beat, milliseconds apart.
But then I started to hear the beat,
the rhythm my heart made, the way it would repeat.
And following the rhythm made me calm down,
it was constant and steady and never broke down.
And so when I panicked, in those moments of fear,
the rhythm of my heart, however severe,
would reassure me that I was OK,
I'd listen to the rhythm and the fear went away.
And so I found music with heavy bass lines,
things with a rhythm made the malignant benign.
So since I was a kid, when things got tough,
I'd go back to the rhythm, poems, music and stuff.
It keeps me away from what I'm thinking,
when my armbands burst, rhythm stops me from sinking.
'Cause it keeps going even when you can't.
It doesn't let you stop, keeps you on a rant.
But sometimes it's harder than others to rhyme
because the words you need don't fit with the time. Signature.
And then I work harder to make it all fit
because if it starts to unravel, the fan fills with shit.
So all of my life when I feel like I'm losing,
or things slip out of control, get scary and confusing,
I go back to the rhyme to keep it together,
so I'm in control, whatever the weather.
And sometimes the rhyme is far-fetched or weak
but as long as it rhymes it's not hard to speak.

It keeps me away from the words in my head,
the ones that don't rhyme, that fill me with dread.
And sometimes it's harder than others to rhyme,
I don't have the words, the strength or the time.
It's like nothing rhymes with the feelings I feel,
I can't distance myself 'cause it's all just too real.

And when the rhyme stops or I can't make it fit,
my heart beats out of time and it's all just a bit

too much to handle – and now I have to use the word candle.
Because then I can breathe and it's not so chaotic,
something, something, something antibiotic.

20
OUCH!

ST ANTHONY AND I HAD BEEN ON THE ROCKS FOR a while before I lost my last two Solpadeine. After I checked inside every pocket in every piece of clothing owned by me and both the Boy and Girl Housemates, and having sticky substances gather under my fingernails as I scraped the bottom of handbags that hadn't been opened in months, I was DONE with him. Things don't just disappear, like. They *had* to be somewhere. Since the restrictions on selling over-the-counter opioids came into place, I had learned that people – in this case pharmacists – let the slightest amount of power go to their heads.

'We won't be dispensing any codeine to you today, miss, would you like some paracetamol?'

'Is that a trick question? They're only a placebo. I have a tooth trying to penetrate my gum, like.'

She knew well that I had no such tooth complaint – and I knew that she knew, so I left. That was the day I realised that pain changes me. Like the TV commercial where people turn back into humans after being monsters on eating a Snickers, getting rid of the constant headache I felt made me feel human. That sort of a dull ache made me agitated and almost aggressive because of its relentlessness.

Pain is relative. The word means something different to everyone. Women talk about forgetting the pain of childbirth after their child is born. It's like some sort of evolutionary conspiracy that alters the memory and changes the perception of how painful it was.

Pain is also relative and reference-dependent. When I was a small child, I stuck my finger into an open socket and experienced mild electrocution. I remember saying it was the worst pain I had ever felt. As I cried, I tried to highlight the severity of the pain by saying that every other time in my few years on the planet that I had said something was sore – grazed knees, tummy aches, missing teeth – they had all been lies because *this* was the worst pain ever.

I never crawled as a child. After I'd learned to pull myself to a standing position, my nana laid Smarties around the room at small intervals in an attempt to encourage me to crawl from one Smartie to the next. Although it was before I had any teeth, it should have been the first sign that I had a sweet tooth and someone should monitor my relationship with sugar. I realised that I would get more sweets if I walked because I would get to them more quickly. Missing the major evolutionary stage of crawling meant that I was a very clumsy child. I was a balance-challenged teenager who spent a disproportionate amount of time in A&E. One year, the doctors had to ask my mother not to bring me back for any more x-rays because I had reached the recommended allowance exposure to radiation for the year.

As a pre-teen, the worst pain I had felt was not a physical pain at all. The discomfort of my little electrocution had been usurped by the pain of a sadness. This feeling was certainly exacerbated by my free-floating, prepubescent hormones, but it was pain nonetheless. The isolating, identity-undermining agony of never being able to find one of those keyrings or emblazoned mugs that they sell at petrol stations with my name on them. My name spelled *correctly*. When they became a big craze, I had teddy bears, keyrings, pens, pencil cases, mugs and the odd snow globe with my name spelled with a *ph*. Stephanie with a *ph* was contemptuous in her promiscuity and pervasiveness, but there was never *Stefanie* with an *f*. Every pit stop for diesel reinforcing a painful identity crisis.

It was the bumps and scrapes and fractures and breaks that made me realise that if you experience a lot of pain, you become used to being in pain and somehow grow a greater level of tolerance for it.

The kneeling rails attached to the pews in the local church in my hometown had lost their padding. Years of parishioners kneeling to tell their sins to Jesus Christ had worn away the spongy comfort, so all we were left with was an exposed piece of unvarnished wood staring at us from behind a frayed leather cover. I told my mother several times that it was painful when I knelt. I didn't have too much cause for kneeling as a child, so I don't blame my mother for thinking I was just trying to get out of praying – it was a complaint that seemed to come around only on a Sunday.

Eventually, one Hallowe'en, on seeing that I also couldn't kneel down to bob for apples during a party, she decided to believe that my issue was not with the Catholic Church but with my knee. When she took me to the doctor, my mother was riddled with guilt – Catholic guilt – when he examined the growth popping out at the top of my shin and diagnosed me with Osgood-Schlatter disease. The pain of him hitting the reflex hammer off my kneecap was the worst pain I've ever felt. Although that new threshold would only remain for two weeks.

My diagnosis meant I had struck gold. I had a doctor's certificate to get me out of PE class indefinitely. Other non-sporty kids saw my doctor's note as a green card to freedom. A green card that excused me not just from pointless games of tag rugby where no one kept score but, more enviably, from afternoons in double English where we congealed in our own stale sweat over the poetry of Patrick Kavanagh. There were no showers in our school so if you worked your heart rate up to a fat-burning level in PE, you had to stew in your own cardiovascular juices for the rest of the day. The sweat collecting dead skin under your damp shirt and woolly jumper.

My PE teacher saw right through me. She knew that I was just delighted to have this medical exemption from her class. She knew that I never wanted to take part and that, at the first sign of a sniffle, I would convince my mother to write me a note. 'Please excuse Stefanie from PE today as she has a chest infection', was scribbled at the bottom corner of my homework diary on almost every page. I won't apologise for my aversion to doing jumping jacks facing the Home Ec. room and I pity any students who fell foul of the fitness bleep test. I tapped my diseased knee lovingly as I sat and watched my peers running in concentric circles and jumping at the sound of an intermittent whistle.

That teacher had resented me for years and saw my condition as a manoeuvre in a battle she needed to win. She redoubled her efforts to make me participate in class. I wouldn't be surprised if she had gone home and googled 'exercises available to people with Osgood-Schlatter disease'.

One Friday in January, our PE teacher made us go for a walk outside the school grounds. Most of the class had that misplaced excitement students get when they are allowed outside the school gates, even though they came in through them that morning. It's as if when you get in the gates, you're never really sure if you'll be allowed back out so the permission is exciting.

The teacher told me I had to go. I reminded her about my exemption. She had all of these statistics ready in an arsenal to throw at me. She said I couldn't be left in the gym unattended and they were going so I had to. She could prove that I could technically walk up to two miles and highlighted that I was happily walking around the school all day and down town for lunch. Checkmate.

I dragged my feet along the concrete footpath at the back of the group. I sulked until I realised she wasn't looking at me and then took out my contraband phone in protest. I was wearing my uniform because I no longer brought PE gear and none of the spare stuff fitted me. I made sure the whole group knew how unhappy I was by strolling so slowly we would be late back for our next class. They all had to go at my pace because, when you take kids out of school, you have to make sure there's never more than an inch between them.

While texting at the back of the herd, I wasn't watching where I was going. I tripped over the uneven concrete where Michael Woodford had left his shoe print and fell straight down onto the road, breaking my arm. The eye-watering immediacy of the pain in my arm shot through me and erased everything else. There was nothing else but me and the pain and the ground. In a way, it was much easier to manage than the pain of resentment, and the embarrassment of doing PE in a skirt, and the discomfort of being the fat kid who needs to find a weekly excuse to get out of running. One big pain is much easier to deal with.

No one believed my arm was broken. My teacher thought I was just making the biggest possible scene because I hadn't wanted to go on the walk in the first place. When I arrived in the following day, with my arm wrapped in a cast, a long line of friends and well-wishers queuing up to sign it, the PE teacher passed me in the hall. I swear I saw a flash of defeat in her eyes. Well, I didn't really know what she was thinking, but I was well-used to those rolling eyeballs, accompanied by an exhale that was an unspoken gesture of 'I give up'.

The story of my fall spread around the school quicker than a guess-who-farted-in-class rumour. By the end of the next day, the anecdote had mutated into a story that involved me getting pushed in front of a car by my teacher. I never corrected any of the adaptations I heard.

I loved the attention that accompanied being the girl in the class who was injured. People opened doors for me, carried my books, wrote down my homework or opened my bottle of water. It was a nice trade-off for the acute pain shooting up and down my arm.

The fractured radius became one break on a long list of breaks that was added to until my late teens. It may have been a cocktail of brittle bones, clumsiness, attention-seeking and daring-to-boldly-go-where-no-child-had-gone-before – like up trees and over walls. Whatever the reason, I spent a large percentage of my childhood with different parts of me wrapped in plaster of Paris.

I learned to manage physical pain with painkillers. I became an expert at knowing how to anticipate the half-life of a Solpadeine. Before I stopped taking codeine-based painkillers, I had learned that I would get three hours and seventeen minutes of pain freedom from two Solpadeine. It was a finely tuned machine, my nervous system.

I found it hard to accept that there were pains that I couldn't numb with painkillers.

Worry pains and cringe pains couldn't be eradicated, despite my best efforts. Cringe pains were always about the past and worry pains were usually triggered by the future. One time, they happened together. It felt like a stomach ulcer and it's painful to even recount ...

I sent a text to the wrong person.

Even worse, I sent a text to the wrong *people*.

Worse again, I sent a text that was inappropriate to the wrong people.

It was inappropriate because of a typo that I didn't even notice until someone's dad called me up about it.

Trying to find a way to describe this story makes my wrists weak. I'm squeezing one eye closed as I type, remembering the moment my words moved from a work-in-progress, easily edited block of text – the vertical line flashing where I had finished, giving me the option of deleting – into an irreversible, un-unseeable, irrevocable bubble of text message permanence.

I used to teach dance and drama classes to children in rural Ireland. On a Wednesday and a Saturday, I would watch the spikey protrusions of high-rise Dublin fade into soft focus and then disappear in my rear-view mirror as the vast flat midlands sprawled in front of me, interrupted only by toll booths and the oddest roadside civic art.

The hip-hop classes I gave to the four-year-olds of Longford were an imported sprinkling of the exotic in a community that had just discovered the spring roll. It would be another fifteen years before the word *avocado* made its way to this sleepy village that seemed to thrive on tradition.

I wasn't sure if the locals would take to the idea of a hip-hop class for kids. The children who attended my class on a Wednesday evening were either coming from or going to fiddle lessons, traditional flute groups or the non-negotiable Irish-dancing class.

I thank the popularity of the TV show *Glee* for sending twenty children my way for two or more years. They would arrive in a convoy from their last extracurricular activity, dressed and ready for me, looking like faraway versions of the supporting cast in a Jane Fonda exercise video. Headbands and leg warmers and everything American television had told them they needed to have to *do* hip-hop.

There are only so many times you can try to teach rhythm to a kid who just doesn't have it. Replaying 'Closer' by Ne-Yo over and over and over hadn't done anything to help Tyler, who I'm fairly sure had dyspraxia. It had, however, sent the rest of the class and me into some hypnotised state of derangement. It was on the sixteenth replay of the song that I understood why eternal repetition of simple chord progressions is used as a form of torture for prisoners of war in internment camps.

Like the boys in Take That in 1996 – we just needed a break from the music. So I started teaching drama in my hip-hop class. The six- to nine-year-olds took to it like you wouldn't believe. The little scenes they made up were couched in high drama and conflicts they had no cultural experience of.

One vignette saw Barry (aged six) and Joanne (aged eight) have a lovers' tiff. She managed to summon actual tears as she shouted at tiny Barry about him leaving her. The word 'baby daddy' was spat at him, and I wondered if these children's entire reality was based on fiction like mine had been. And if that was the case, did I have a responsibility to tell their parents that their fictional influences may need to be reconsidered? I decided to leave it. I had enough going on.

They were hip-hop kids, or Ireland's version of that. They were understandably having a hard time separating the lyrics they were listening to from the lives they were living in rural Longford. When Joanne started quoting the old R 'N' B song by City High, I took it as a cue to start working on scripted scenes with them.

She wasn't happy to have been interrupted mid-chorus, as she was singing her heart out about the woman who slept with men to feed her crying and hungry son. (The melody was catchy, but the lyrics were pretty dark.)

I bought a small cheap Nokia phone to use for my classes. I was earnestly trying to avoid the very incident I'm about to describe.

The little Nokia brick had predictive text and a game of snake and that was all I needed to run the class. I would text the parents of the kids on the day of the class and remind them to bring anything specific. As I said, they were busy packing SUVs full of fiddles and flutes and football boots so the reminder was appreciated.

On the Wednesday morning, I stood in a printing shop in Dublin with the brick phone in one hand and the warm A4 pages straight out of the printer in the other. I sent a text to all the parents. One big group message, as usual.

What I wanted the text to say was:

> Hey, guys, please don't forget to send the kids in in costume today as I'll be bringing the new scripts. See you later. Stef.

On Nokia phones, predictive text means that the combination of numbers you press may create several different words and you have to press the *down* button to select the correct one. The word *scripts* has the same number combinations as another word which comes before it alphabetically and therefore shows up first.

The message I sent to the twenty mothers and fathers of my children's hip-hop group in rural Ireland said:

> Hey, guys, please don't forget to send the kids in in costume today as I'll be bringing the new rapists. See you later. Stef.

It was a combination of the typo and the time elapsed before spotting it that did the damage.

I didn't even notice.

It wasn't until Barry's father called me that I realised something was up. Barry's father and I had had an unspoken awkwardness since day one *anyway*. Barry's dad arrived early, presumably to lump me with his kid for longer so he could go and do whatever dads do when they are child-free. I wasn't expecting him to walk by the window, and I made direct eye contact with him while I was adjusting my bra. It was innocent, I was fully clothed and just needed a reconfiguration after the drive, but it was enough to douse all subsequent interactions with a heavy sprinkling of unspoken cringe.

We danced around the typo for a while because I didn't know

there had been any mistake. I was confused by his confusion, which was making him annoyed because he thought I was trying to be funny or something.

When I re-read what I had said while on the phone to him I just wanted to be dead. I wanted to run out of the printer's and into oncoming traffic. I wanted to set myself on fire. The pain of the discomfort of the misunderstanding was so unbearable that I wanted to cause actual physical targeted pain to myself because at least then I would be able to focus on an injury and nurse it back to health – that would have been easier than trying to wriggle out of my own skin with the nebulous, hard-to-reach shame that was building inside me. The queue for the printer was building and my lot had all landed in the paper tray. I'm sure people were asking me to move on, but all I could hear was my heart racing in my chest as I tried to do the impossible and undo the past.

My brain kicked into overdrive and I did what I always do. I called my friend Rachel. 'Rach, I sent a text to a load of parents saying I was bringing rapists to their kids and could they please send them to me in costume.'

'What?'

'I sent a text to a load of parents saying I was bringing rapists to their kids and could they please send them to me in costume.' I repeated at the same speed and tone. 'What do I do? WHAT DO I DO?'

Rachel calmed me down enough to type a message that she dictated that acknowledged the typo but didn't make a big deal out of it.

Sorry about that. Predictive text. I will have the SCRIPTS with me, see you all at 5.

I spent the rest of the day and the entire drive to the midlands with a worry pain inside me the size of a grapefruit. Heavy and sour in the pit of my stomach. Sometimes, I would be distracted enough to forget *what* I was worried about but the pain would still be there.

I didn't see them all at five. Only half the kids were there. I reassured myself that *Glee* became passé in middle Ireland on that Wednesday, before anywhere else in the world, and that's why people stopped coming, and *not* because of my misspelled text message.

Barry's dad was still the first to arrive, ready to drop his son fifteen minutes early so he could 'get to the bookies'. Bets before threats, I guess. None of the parents said anything to me about the text, which was nearly worse even though that's what I had prayed would happen.

I wished I had one of those *Men in Black* mind-eraser tools.

They waited just long enough to make me question their motivation before pulling their kids out of the class. I told myself that I didn't mind, really. The midlands just wasn't ready for my hip-hop-theatre hybrid. The truth was, I minded very much. I had lost my class, my dignity and potentially my garda-vetting clearance to work with young people.

As I drove back to Dublin, the shame of my typo keeping pace with my car and the speed limit, I felt the familiar niggle start at my temples. The stress was causing a headache that only one thing could fix. I pulled into a pharmacy somewhere west of Enfield and jumped through the usual codeine hoops. As the hope effervesced in the bottom of my Volvic bottle, I took a moment to strategise how to get back all of the things I had lost.

When the fizzing had stopped and the water went clear, I swallowed my pride and my painkillers and said one final prayer to St Anthony.

21
LOOKING FORWARD TO CHANGE

I ONCE HEARD THAT IN A FILM, PLAY OR BOOK, 'People will forgive anything except a bad ending'. Naturally, I don't want to walk away from my first book having committed a mortal sin, so I turned to my mentor and dear friend in a panic.

'I don't know how to end my book.'

She came back immediately with, 'It should not contain a moral or a dismissal.'

So, because I am obedient and thrive on obeying the rules

I am presented with, the following summation is intended to contain no moral or dismissal.

Please do not get confused by the title of this chapter. I have not suddenly become an impulsive and spontaneous nomad, ready to take on all the surprises life throws at me with glee and gusto simply because I have written a book. There's no life-altering conclusions to draw. Funnily enough, not much has changed in the last 280 or so pages. Except … that I have become acutely aware that change is inevitable and I am now faced with the scary reality that I haven't experienced my quota of change yet. When I look forward to the future, without being Nostradamus or anything, I can objectively see more change coming.

I am going to get older.

There will be more birthdays.

I will presumably, ideally, have children.

I will presumably, ideally, lie to them about Santa.

More people I love will die.

New people for me to love will be born.

There will be career successes that plunge me more into the public eye.

I will make wrong choices and some people's opinions of me will change.

I will outgrow my mentor.

I will lose touch with friends.

I will make new friends.

I may get married.

My car will change, my clothes will change, I will go grey.

There may be a new currency.

There may be no EU.

My passport will expire.

My bank account figures will fluctuate.

More terrorism will happen.

I will vote and have people I either love or hate dictating policy to me from Government Buildings.

I will look back at this book and cringe at my naiveté.

The Boy Housemate will move out or move on.

There will be new social media platforms.

Children will make references that I don't understand and I will feel old.

Polar ice caps will continue to melt.

The price of fossil fuels will rise.

Cars will drive themselves.

Everyone will have to be a Deliveroo driver.

New brands of food will be invented.

Species will become extinct.

Avocados will go out of fashion.

My book will be on shelves.

I will have sleepless nights.

Everywhere will be Starbucks.

People will forget who Sabrina the Teenage Witch was.

They may stop showing *Friends* every day.

The Charlie-bit-my-finger kid will have kids of his own.

Someone else will have a weight-loss story.

I will forget the names of the people who win this year's *X-Factor*.

Virtual reality will become normal.

The iPhone 8 will become obsolete.

People who aren't even born yet will make scientific discoveries that discount what we now believe to be an absolute truth.

I will have to get a solicitor.

I will have to make appointments I'm afraid to make.

There is only one way for me to avoid all of these changes and that is to not take part in life.

But weighing it all up … I'd rather opt in than opt out, and even though I might not *like* change, it turns out I might be better at coping with it than I thought. And if not – there'll always be grown-ups around to pick me up, brush me off and send me back into the world no matter what age I am.

ACKNOWLEDGEMENTS
(IN ALPHABETICAL ORDER)

- Aileen (for making sure people know about the book).
- Cathal (for fixing bits before anyone had a chance to spot them).
- Ciara and team Hachette (for the belief and the edits).
- Clara (for being the voice of reason).
- Jo (for her lists and plans and style).
- Lorcan (for knowing the questions before people ask them).
- Mam (for the Bisto bits).
- Matthew (for holding my heart and hand)
- Marc, David and Jasmine (for helping me to cope).
- Nana (for all the lessons).
- Nell and Amy (for reading it first).
- Rachel (for being my twin).
- Rob, Emmett and Diarmuid from Himiko Productions (for the short film adaptations).
- Sarah (for the make-up skills).

- Terry and Tom (for being my grown-ups).
- The man who sat in seat 24A on a flight from Dublin to New York (for lending me his laptop charger so I could make my deadline for this book).

I also want to acknowledge that I change my mind all the time. One day, I love natural yoghurt; the next, I'm dairy free. Don't hold me to anything I've said in this book. When you have read it, erase it from your mind and never mention it – please.

Some of the stories in this book have been adapted, amended for legal reasons or embellished because it wasn't as interesting to other people as it is to me. Parts of some of them have also appeared in *The Sunday Independent LIFE Magazine*.

To anyone who has lived by 'If you don't have anything nice to say don't say anything at all', I look forward to our silent meetings down the line.

Stef